ADAM SMITH'S

THE WEALTH
OF NATIONS

ADAM SMITH'S

THE WEALTH
OF NATIONS

TIMELESS Concepts for TODAY

CALUM ROBERTS

This edition published in 2011 by

Media Eight International Publishing Limited

3 Linkside, New Malden,
Surrey KT3 4LA, United Kingdom

Tel: +44 (0)20 8605 1097

ISBN: 978-81-7314-258-1

Printed in India by Gopsons Papers Ltd

CONTENTS

INTRODUCTION

When Scottish moral philosopher and economist Adam Smith finished his opus, most probably he didn't realise that it would become a landmark examination of political economy. Published in 1776, *The Wealth of Nations* details the benefits, interconnections and consequences of a free-market economy that paved the way for modern capitalism. Smith believed that there could be no market for anything unless someone, somewhere, was willing to pay for it. He was convinced of the merits of a laissez-faire (let-the-market-decide) approach because he believed competition, not intervention, would naturally regulate the market and thus some 'invisible hand' would ensure justice and equality for all.

For example, Smith was of the view that a free market would make monopoly impossible and therefore workers and consumers could not be exploited. If over-demand for a certain product existed, then that demand would naturally encourage others to compete in the same market and prices would fall. By default, this competitive environment would also improve innovation and quality.

Smith offers a thorough exposé of business from an economic and social perspective and it is clear that he has also given a great deal of thought to the ethics of business, although his most detailed work on the subject was contained in *The Theory of Moral Sentiment*, published seventeen years earlier. It is perhaps this consideration for such topics that makes his study so special: he doesn't just offer an incisive look at finance, economics and politics – he does so within the context of ethics, philosophy and historical fact. As a consequence, *The Wealth of Nations* has become a classic and Smith is still widely referenced today.

There are five separate books that make up *The Wealth of Nations*. The first three explore the division of labour, origins of money and the importance of wages, profit, rent and stocks. Book four examines the mercantile system, looking specifically at the British Colonies, while book five develops the case for restricted state involvement and describes how to fund education, transport, justice and defence.

To settle on just 52 key points from such a breadth of information was difficult; it would have been just as easy to choose three times as many. Consequently this is by no means a substitute to the original work. It is, however, a useful addendum as it brings many of Smith's thoughts to life through modern-day examples, events and financial stories. In narrowing down my focus, I have therefore chosen to concentrate on getting key ideas across while also offering insights that have a particular, if not somewhat ironic relevance today.

Adam Smith is considered the father of 'classical' economics and his contribution to the subject is similar to what Darwin did for science. In many ways Smith's famous book is an evolution of industry and explains how commerce emerged and incrementally improved over time. The ideas are solid, sensible and logical, and yet as time has progressed way beyond his death in 1790, the execution of that theory, as is so often the case, would probably make the canny Scot spin in his grave. In its purest sense, his capitalist vision does have advantages and has produced many great and noble consequences, but I can't help but wonder what Mr Smith would make of the excesses of capitalism we've witnessed in the twenty-first century. My guess is that he might wish that he had added a little more emphasis on the importance of a strong moral and ethical compass, if the benefits of a free economy are to be reaped without making room for the exploitation and evil that has been such an unfortunate by-product.

HOW TO INCREASE PRODUCTIVITY

Often he who does too much does too little.
- ITALIAN PROVERB

Smith believed that the division of labour, breaking processes down to their smallest task and having one person perfect that task, led to increased dexterity and output. He uses the example of a nail maker and describes how with practice the dexterity of the nail maker would improve to the point where if he exerted himself he could make, 'upwards of two thousand three hundred nails a day'. What fun!

The process also improved performance. If a worker was only doing one job, then no time was wasted in moving from one task to another. Smith notes, *'The habit of sauntering and of indolent careless application by workmen obliged to change his work and his tools every half hour renders him almost always slothful and lazy and incapable of any vigorous application even on the most pressing occasion.'*

Most probably, he would be very impressed with modern business and the efficiencies brought about by technology. However, that same technology is a double-edged sword. We may save time and travel expense on conference calls and we might have the tools to switch

---

FOOD FOR THOUGHT

If you manage a team and want to find out how to increase productivity and efficiency, then encourage your staff to improve their own processes. The people doing the jobs are always those best placed to improve them. Make it known that you are creating a monthly innovation prize. Each month employees are invited to contribute their ideas about how to improve productivity in their area. Every idea that makes or saves the business money is implemented and the inventor wins a cash prize.

WORDS OF WISDOM

Adam Smith starts by exploring improvement, attributing it to, 'the increase of dexterity; to the saving of the time which is commonly lost in passing from one species of work to another; and to the invention of a great number of machines which facilitate one man to do the work of many'.

---

projects and change tasks without too much 'sauntering', but there are now many more traps to capture minds in unproductive work, whether that's a sneaky game of Tetris on the spare office computer, checking your emails for the fourteenth time in two hours or sending inane messages to people on Facebook. According to Peninsula, an employment law firm, employees waste 233 million hours on social networking sites at an estimated cost to UK business of £130 million a day!

Smith also points out that, 'Men are much more likely to discover easier methods when the whole attention of their mind is directed towards that single object than when it is dissipated among a great variety of things.' This focused attention on a single task brings natural improvement as the worker seeks to simplify the process and make it easier for them to achieve the outcome.

As the name suggests, the Industrial Revolution transformed industry but it wasn't much fun for most of those involved in it! It's all very well to become a specialist and to know more and more about less and less, and certainly specialisation is useful and in many professions such as brain surgery it's certainly comforting, but too much specialisation must have been mind-numbing, back-breaking work.

YOUR THOUGHTS

THE SOURCES
OF INVENTION

Discovery consists of seeing what everyone
has seen and thinking what nobody has thought.
- ALBERT GYORGYI,
Nobel Prize Winner

Apparently a boy was constantly employed in the first fire engines to open and shut the communication between boiler and cylinder as a piston went up and down. One inventive young lad, who preferred playing to working, noticed that if he simply tied a string to the handle then the piston would open and shut the valve without his assistance, 'and leave him at liberty to divert himself with his play-fellows'.

Smith goes on to suggest that other inventions are made by, '*philosophers or men of speculation, whose trade it is not to do anything, but to observe everything; and who, upon that account, are often capable of combining together the powers of the most distant and dissimilar objects*'.

Just look at the humble laser. Albert Einstein's ability to combine distant and dissimilar objects led to his groundbreaking observation of Max Planck's Law of Radiation. It was 'Einstein's coefficients' in 1917 that laid the foundation for the invention of the laser. Forty years later, Charles Hard Townes and Arthur Leonard Schawlow invented the concept, but

---
FOOD FOR THOUGHT

When a new employee joins the team they are usually keen to exert their influence and make their mark. Those with experience in other businesses or industries either cross-pollinate good ideas into a new business or end up throwing the baby out with the bathwater. Upon arrival, initiate a group brainstorming session to bring existing and new ideas together, and choose the best in a collaborative and supportive way.

WORDS OF WISDOM

They say necessity is the mother of invention. Adam Smith believed that laziness, or at least self-interest, was the father. He talks of the fire engine and of how, 'one of the greatest improvements since it was first invented was the discovery of a boy who wanted to save his own labour'.

---

they were pipped at the post: the first working laser was demonstrated by Theodore Maiman at Hughes Research Laboratories, California, in May 1960.

Since then laser technology has been adopted into a wide range of unrelated businesses because someone was able to see beyond its current use, tweak the technology and move it into new fields. Today lasers are used in industries as diverse as optical storage in CDs and DVDs, fibre optic communication, bar codes, laser printers, and in medicine, with bloodless surgery, laser healing and eye correction. The same basic technology is also employed in manufacturing for cutting and welding, while the beauty industry uses lasers for hair removal and to treat acne. In the military, lasers are used for range finding, target designation, even testing directed energy weapons. Laser lighting is also used in entertainment, such as the laser light show, the Symphony of Lights, that takes place over Hong Kong every night at 8 p.m.

Smith reminds us that invention is possible by those at the coalface of operation when, 'each individual becomes more expert in his own peculiar branch, more work is done upon the whole, and the quantity of science is considerably increased by it'. It is also possible for those sufficiently removed from the process to pull in knowledge from other areas and make connections not previously seen by others.

YOUR THOUGHTS

THE IMPORTANCE
OF INTUITION

Often you have to rely on intuition.
- BILL GATES,
Microsoft Billionaire

Granted the people involved in the development of the laser probably didn't foresee its 'extensive utility'. Einstein, however, was known for his strong belief in intuition, a mysterious and illusive aspect of 'human wisdom' that Smith makes no reference to.

The challenge with any theory that involves human beings is regardless of how logical it appears on paper, when it's translated into life the wheels can fall off! The things that make us human also render us difficult to predict and systemise. In addition, there are mysterious aspects of human nature that we still don't understand, intuition being one of them.

When Garry Kasparov, Russian World Chess Champion, started playing chess against the IBM computer they were evenly matched – both could predict four to five moves ahead. Deep Blue, however, was a computer and kept learning until eventually they played their final match in 1997, when Deep Blue could predict millions of potential moves in under a minute, making it theoretically far superior. The media went crazy when Deep Blue won 3½ to 2½. What's extraordinary about that result,

---
FOOD FOR THOUGHT

Science may not be able to explain intuition but most people won't deny that it exists. There's something very powerful about the instinctive gut feeling, whether it's an initial response to a new acquaintance or a feeling about which course of action to take. Trust your intuition before anything else. Forget facts, figures and statistics, forget complex formulae and calculations; forget recommendations and testimonials: if you have a bad feeling about something, don't do it!

though, is not that the computer beat the World Champion, but that
Kasparov won any games at all! And the only explanation is intuition.

The problem is that intuition isn't an exact science and as such, business
largely ignores it – at least officially. In a lecture at the Massachusetts
Institute of Technology (MIT) on 22 September 2005, 'Leading By
Omission', Brazilian businessmen and corporate innovator Ricardo
Semler told the audience about his experience of intuition in big business.
Semler visited the head planner for a major oil company and discovered
that while his personal log of intuitive forecasts was consistently more
accurate than the complex, yet accepted mathematical and research
based tools he never shared those findings with the board, even though
they might have saved the oil company billions. The head planner
recognised that telling the board of directors that he was basing his
five-year forecasts on a hunch would be a career limiting move, adding,
'I've been here thirty years and have earned the right to be wrong but
I have to be precisely wrong to guarantee my survival.'

Financial legends and famous inventors often confess to the importance
of intuition in their success, however this is usually in retrospect.
Admitting to intuitive prowess is a luxury only the successful can afford.
Society in general, and business in particular, does not yet officially
accept intuition as the powerful human advantage it truly is.

--- YOUR THOUGHTS ---

MARKETS CAN BE MANIPULATED

*An important scientific innovation rarely makes
its way by gradually winning over and converting
its opponents. What does happen is that its opponents
gradually die out, and that the growing generation is
familiarized with the ideas from the beginning.*
- MAX PLANCK,
Founder of Quantum Theory

For a start, the innovation that occurs is often limited to a system already created. Take the automotive industry, for example – industry-wide emulation ensures that despite over 100 years of assembly-line production and billions spent in research and development, the car hasn't actually changed that much.

In 1977 President Jimmy Carter prophetically warned the US that, 'we simply must balance our need for energy with our rapidly shrinking resources'. But no one listened, they didn't want to: America was the Land of Plenty and Carter's encouragement toward a less materialistic society lost him the presidency.

What's interesting, though, is that at least a partial solution to his concerns already existed. Fourteen years earlier, in 1963, the German car company Daimler Benz invented an electric car capable of fifty-three miles per day, which even now would probably be enough for 80% of car users. In the early 70s Japan's Honda invented a solution for a hybrid car, while French company Renault produced a solution for an electric car in the 80s. So, why were these innovations not brought to

---

FOOD FOR THOUGHT

If you are in business, encourage people to question everything. Take the time to consciously assess your policies and procedures – 'Because it's always been done that way' isn't a good enough reason to maintain the status quo. Encourage creativity and innovation across the board.

market? Because markets can be manipulated!

Perhaps if people had listened to Jimmy Carter in the 70s and had been presented with the facts and repercussions, Vice President Al Gore wouldn't have had to create *An Inconvenient Truth* in 2006. Had the governments even then got behind the existing science and helped people to really understand the impact of their actions, perhaps the market would have been created. Instead, and especially in the US, government was consistently populated by those with vested interests in oil and the status quo.

Beyond any Oliver Stone-style conspiracies, however, human nature must be considered. It is very difficult to change something from the inside – our compulsion to keep doing what we've always done is very strong. Social psychologist Robert Cialdini refers to this as, 'commitment and consistency', and believes that we are driven to remain consistent with our past decisions and actions, even when they are obviously wrong. Another influencing factor is 'social proof', which refers to safety in numbers and how we are influenced by what others do. If everyone in the automotive, or indeed any other industry, has been doing something a certain way for a long time then there is huge resistance toward change. Being collectively wrong is better and safer than being individually wrong!

YOUR THOUGHTS

HABIT CREATES TALENT

*Everyone according to their talent and
every talent according to its work.*
- FRENCH PROVERB

According to Smith talent is not the result of nature or nurture. The differences only emerged when, *'about that age, or soon after they come to be employed in very different occupations'*. The difference of talents becomes noticeable until, *'at last the vanity of the philosopher is willing to acknowledge scarce any resemblance'*.

First of all, it's hard to imagine that a person's 'career' would begin at the age of six or eight. Can you imagine the kids you know of that age doing anything but playing? And yet, in Smith's time, children as young as six were working pistons on fire engines, pulling coal carks up mine shafts and doing long shifts in textile mills. It would be forty-three years after Smith's death before any legislation protecting children was passed. The Factory Act of 1833 outlawed children younger than nine from the textile industry and limited the length of shifts, as well as setting out provisions for education. Still, it was a very tough life.

Smith suggests there is very little to differentiate one child from another and it was purely down to luck and circumstance whether you ended up a philosopher or a street sweeper. The same is probably true today and certainly the snobbery between the two is alive and well.

FOOD FOR THOUGHT
If you have kids or work with children, look out for the little clues. Keep a record of the things they say – apart from anything else, this will be great fodder for their twenty-first birthday party speech. What do they say they want to do when they grow up? Make a note of the subtle differences so that you can tell them in later life. Often these clues can be helpful in steering a child into a profession that will make them happy.

The current education system does not cater for the identification of
talents that may sit outside Maths, English or Science. Luckily there are
moves toward this goal, although it will probably be many decades
before it makes its way into mainstream teaching. The Theory of
Multiple Intelligences was developed in 1983. Dr Howard Gardner,
Hobbs Professor of Cognition and Education at Harvard suggested
measuring intelligence based on IQ was far too limited. Instead he
proposed eight different intelligences to account for the broad range
of human potential:

- Verbal – Linguistic Intelligence (Reading)
- Logical – Mathematical Intelligence (Maths)
- Visual – Spatial Intelligence (Art)
- Bodily – Kinesthetic Intelligence (Building)
- Musical Intelligence (Music)
- Interpersonal Intelligence (Working Together)
- Intrapersonal Intelligence (Personal Work)
- Naturalistic Intelligence (Nature).

Dr Gardner's work demonstrates the depth and breath of individual
talent and suggests we all have innate differences that can offer clues
to our abilities and potential careers. Perhaps if we were more open to
these subtle indications at an early age, people would be better able
to find jobs and careers that made them truly happy rather than simply
paid the bills.

YOUR THOUGHTS

DIVERSIFY INTO NICHE MARKET

Diversify or Die.
- ANON

Smith was writing his economic treatise just as mass production looked set to rule the world. If a market was too small, there was no point in creating a specialised product that could not be sustained by that market – in those situations, the craftsmen must diversify. Ironically, the advice is still valid today, but for different reasons.

The Industrial Revolution moved seamlessly into globalisation. The one-size-fits-all approach to business arrived and companies such as McDonald's and Wal-Mart flourished in that environment. Globalisation and technological advances meant that markets traditionally limited by distance opened up and consumers entered a truly global economy. Economies of scale, where large multinationals use their buying muscle to negotiate lower costs ensured prices to the customer were kept low. The downside was that this drove out the competition because smaller suppliers couldn't match the prices and went out of business. This phenomenon can be seen on any high street as more and more small retailers are forced out of business by out-of-town supermarkets selling everything from clothes to insurance.

--- FOOD FOR THOUGHT ---

What are your core skills? Besides your current clients, who else might use those skills? Could you repackage your offer to talk directly to niche audiences? For example, I wrote a book detailing how to become a published author and how doing so can massively impact on your career and income. Being an author is a powerful marketing and business development tool. On the assumption that some readers might never find the time to write their own book and contact me, I focused on a niche.

WORDS OF WISDOM

Adam Smith states that in a small market the division of labour and specialisation is pointless. A carpenter, for example, can't just be a carpenter, *'but a joiner, cabinet-maker, and even a carver in wood, as well as a wheel-wright, a plough-wright, a cart and wagon maker'*. He must diversify or go broke.

But things shifted. Consumers became a little more discerning and stopped responding so enthusiastically to cookie-cutter solutions. They wanted to feel as though their particular situation was being addressed by a tailor-made answer and the need for more sophisticated marketing emerged.

Fact is, you may be selling the same product or service but now you need to sell it with a little more finesse. Smith suggested that specialisation was pointless in a small market because essentially there was a limited demand. Ironically, we've come full circle and that specialisation is now mandatory if you are to effectively compete in the very large market. Appealing to the mass market doesn't work; we can't be all things to all people. Instead, we must identify our key skills and package them up to meet the demands of a variety of niche groups.

For example, I am a writer. That basic skill could be used in a wide range of areas, from website content, business report writing, technical writing to copy writing and ghosting books. I specialise in ghosting books for busy professionals because I enjoy it, but also because saying I'm a writer and can write anything is a weak marketing pitch. This may be true, but it doesn't win business: I have to specialise to succeed, and so do most other businesses.

YOUR THOUGHTS

_____

_____

_____

_____

OPEN UP NEW MARKETS

The more we exploit nature, the more our options are
reduced, until we have only one: to fight for survival.
- MORRIS K. UDALL,
American Politician

Smith doesn't mention 'economies of scale', what he refers to is the improvements in transportation that gave industry many benefits. These included greater efficiencies and cost savings made possible by expansion.

Smith asks, 'What goods could bear the expense of land-carriage between London and Calcutta?' The answer was, and remains not many. It is evident from his writings that he saw transportation by water as a significant improvement to industry. I wonder what he would make of air-travel today?

Opening up new markets and seeking appropriate savings are all part of modern business – but at what price? What cost to those being exploited and paid a pittance for their labour in countries far from where the goods will eventually be sold? What cost to the environment as the carbon footprint of those economic decisions continues to pollute the planet? What cost to land plundered for profit without regard for future generations?

In the 1930s, US industrial farming came of age. Escalating cereal prices

---

FOOD FOR THOUGHT

If your business is being squeezed on price, consider changing your competitive strategy. You will never compete with large business on price alone, so find an alternative way to differentiate yourself. What other aspects of your product or service could you emphasise in order to create a competitive edge? Perhaps you could draw potential customers' attention to environmental credentials or craftsmanship.

attracted profiteers to a traditional small-scale, family-run business not exactly known for its excessive revenue opportunities! In 1931, Hickman Price abandoned his $50,000 salary from Fox Film Corps in Hollywood to buy up 25,000 acres in the Texas Panhandle. Two hundred and fifty mobile maintenance units kept twenty-five silver combines working round the clock and hundreds of trucks ferried the wheat to market. This was 'farming' on a scale previously unseen, with devastating consequences. For a start, the inevitable over-supply depressed prices and sent many, including Mr Hollywood, broke. Worse still was the environmental consequences of removing the prairie grass to make way for acres of wheat when droughts and twisters destroyed the land. On 14 April 1935 an estimated 300,000 tons of flying dirt darkened the skies, from east Colorado to Washington DC. Five days later, Roosevelt's soil conservationist Hugh Bennett implored a Congressional Committee to restore the integrity of the prairie grass before it was too late, pointing to the sullied windows of the Capitol, 'This gentlemen, is what I'm talking about. There goes Oklahoma.'

Smith was excited about the possibilities for business as transportation opened up new markets and made it possible to transport and sell excess goods to new locations for additional profit. But it must be tempered. Perhaps it's time for modern business to adopt the Hippocratic Oath stating, 'First Do No Harm'.

─── YOUR THOUGHTS ───

THE ORIGIN OF MONEY

All government, indeed every human benefit
and enjoyment, every virtue, and every prudent
act, is founded on compromise and barter.
- EDMUND BURKE,
Political Theorist and Philosopher

Economies are developed when people exchange, *'the surplus part of their own labour for such parts of the produce of other men's labour'.* Smith talks of how that exchange took place. Initially, 'cattle were the common instrument of commerce; though they must have been a most inconvenient one'. Certainly, if you were to hand over a cow at your local supermarket, the cashier might be a little perturbed. It's also rather messy to halve a cow and they don't readily fit into one's pocket!

Over the years, many commodities have been used as a means of exchange, including salt, sugar, tobacco and even dried cod. Smith tells of, *'A village in Scotland where it is not uncommon for a workman to carry nails instead of money to the baker's shop or the alehouse.'* Good news for the nail maker on page 3, I suppose!

All of these commodities had their challenges and money emerged as the smart alternative, but even that caused problems. First, there was the issue of weighing the gold and silver. A small variation could make a

---

FOOD FOR THOUGHT

In truth, money is only useful because it allows you to buy things. There's nothing to stop you swapping your goods and services for others that you need from other businesses. Check out Bartercard (www.bartercard.com), which allows you to trade with 55,000 businesses in twelve countries using your own goods and services instead of cash. It's a smart way to get what you need without spending money!

big difference to the value. The second problem was forgery. Covering heavy metals with gold or slicing little bits off each coin before passing it on were common practices. The little shavings would then be melted down to create new coins. It was this action that led to the serrated edge we see on coins today as it eliminated any tampering. *'Hence the origin of coined money, and those public offices called mints... to ascertain, by means of a public stamp, the quality and uniform goodness.'*

Today, the value of money is built on trust rather than any real intrinsic value of the money itself, although in 2006 the price of copper topped $9000 a tonne, which led to fears that people would start to melt down their copper coins as pre-1992 coppers were then worth twice their face value. Considering the Royal Mint estimates that 6.5 billion coppers are missing from circulation in the UK, that's a tidy little profit. Whether you might be bothered to retrieve the estimated £26 million lying in the street, £11 million languishing at the bottom of handbags, £7.8 million stuffed in car ashtrays and glove compartments, and £5.9 million down the back of sofas is quite another matter! According to the Royal Mint, the lost pennies weigh 22,000 tonnes – the same as a decent sized Royal Navy battleship!

YOUR THOUGHTS

WHAT IS 'VALUE'?

Value is the most invincible and impalpable
of ghosts, and comes and goes unthought of whilst
the visible and dense matter remains as it was.
- W. STANLEY JEVONS,
Economist and Philosopher

Smith reminds us, 'the things which have the greatest value in use have frequently little or no value in exchange; and, on the contrary, those which have the greatest value in exchange have frequently little or no value in use'.

He gives the examples of water and diamonds to illustrate his point that nothing is more useful than water, yet nothing much can be exchanged for it. Diamonds, on the other hand, have no value in use, but have huge value in exchange. However, this observation isn't strictly true anymore as diamonds have properties that make them exceptionally useful: they are the hardest natural substance and as such are found in cutting equipment, where durability is essential.

What is perhaps most interesting, though, is the changeable nature of value. If you had dragged yourself out of the desert after five days, what would you value more: diamonds or water? Water is by far the cheapest commodity and yet it is one of the few things we can't live without. Most of us can easily live without diamonds! The irony about Smith's examples is that 'need' against 'want' is highlighted, and the subsequent

---
FOOD FOR THOUGHT

What do you value above all else? Make a list of the ten things in your life for which you are most grateful. You may be surprised to discover that few, if any, relate to money. When the economy turns south and the press is filled with predictions of impending doom and gloom, this may be worth remembering.

potential for exploitation.

When James Bond starts tackling the subject in fiction, perhaps we should all be a little nervous about fact! In the 2008 Bond movie, *Quantum of Solace*, the villain attempts to corner the world's water supplies to sell to the highest bidder. This might seem like fiction now, but perhaps it's already begun with the partial privatisation of water.

It will be interesting to see if the water supply, an industry already worth billions in the bottled variety, will go the same way as energy and hold many households to ransom. Putting what we 'want' in the hands of the free market makes economic sense, while putting what we 'need' in those same hands could prove very dangerous indeed. Surely some commodities, such as food and water, must have the supply protected for all – regardless of financial resources?

As economies expand and contract, it's easier to see the changing nature of value more clearly as our needs take priority over wants. Faced with water or diamonds, even Coca-Cola®, we may end up preferring water. Financial restriction and desperation has a way of levelling our desires and forcing us back toward simplicity.

—— YOUR THOUGHTS ——

THE NEED FOR
BANKING REGULATION

*I hate banks. They do nothing positive for anyone
except take care of themselves. They're first in with
their fees and first out when there's trouble.
- HARVEY GOLDSMITH,
British Music Promoter*

Today's banks may not pay in sixpences but they have created
new and 'interesting' ways to evade immediate payment. Take, for
example, the cheque clearing cycle.

In 2000, a government-appointed banking review led by Don
Cruickshank highlighted, among other things, cheque-clearing times.
According to Cruickshank the system was run like a 'cartel', meaning
the banks joined forces to proliferate a united explanation as to why
it took up to ten days to clear a cheque. Meanwhile, it was estimated
the banks made up to $30 million in interest by 'evading immediate
payment' through the clearing system.

Even the then Governor of the Bank of England, Mervyn King, expressed
'disappointment' at the time it took for cheques and electronic payments
to be cleared. The problem is now partly resolving itself as cheque
usage declines. In 1999, 2.8 billion cheques were written and that figure
is expected to fall to 1.7 billion in 2009.

The Office of Fair Trading in the UK also became involved and, as of

---

FOOD FOR THOUGHT

Even with increased government guarantees, you need to ensure all
your savings eggs are not in one basket. Divide them up across different
banking institutions to make sure they are not part of the same group.
Remember, a bank may have a different high-street name but be owned
by the same group and compensation will only apply per group.

November 2007, money paid into an account by cheque now starts to earn interest, or be offset against an overdraft, within two working days, rather than three.

Smith went on to say that banks, *'would be obliged to keep at all times in their coffers a greater quantity of cash than at present; and though this might no doubt be a considerable inconveniency to them, it would at the same time be a considerable security to their creditors'.*

Following the banking difficulties of late 2008, few creditors felt any considerable security about their savings, so much so that the Financial Services Authority (FSA) increased the compensation limit on saving deposits from £35,000 to £50,000 in an effort to calm a nervous public.

According to Smith, *'the coffers of the bank resemble a pond, from which though a stream is continually running out, yet another stream is continually running in, fully equal to that which runs out; so that, without any further care or attention, the pond keeps always equally, or very nearly equally full'.* Yet in modern times this didn't happen... Apparently during the height of the lending frenzy, US banks lent $30 for every $1 held in deposits. In the UK and Europe the ratio was $50:$1, while in Australia, tighter regulation limited it to $13:$1. Meanwhile, in Iceland a staggering $300 was 'running out' for every $1 'running in'!

──────── YOUR THOUGHTS ────────

HOW TO MAKE MONEY

*Differentiate your products, provide great
service and don't even think about trying to
compete with Wal-Mart on price.
- MICHAEL BERGDAHL,
Former Wal-Mart Executive*

To make money, something has to be sold – what, how, when, where and for how much is all part of the business puzzle. Price, therefore, is a large part of that puzzle and getting it right is essential to success. When working out the price of goods or services, the merchant must take into consideration all costs associated with its creation, including the wages of labour to make it, the rent of any land or buildings where that item was created and the level of profit he or she wishes to make.

These issues now come under the topic of competitive strategy. And in modern business it is leading authority Michael Porter, professor at Harvard Business School, who has put business strategy firmly on the corporate board table. Porter offers three generic strategies for gaining competitive advantage relating directly to what Smith talks about regarding price:

- Cost leadership – be the lowest-cost producer because buyers like a bargain
- Differentiation – be different so you can justify higher prices

---
FOOD FOR THOUGHT

Competing on price alone is a dangerous strategy, especially when the economy contracts. If you have a new product or service, test the price with your market before launching it. A great way to do this cost effectively is to use pay-per-click advertising online. Create alternative prices and test the response – you may find that sales are not affected by price as much as you imagine. Find out, don't guess, what the market will bear!

WORDS OF WISDOM

Adam Smith writes that the price of commodities resolves itself into one or other of three parts: wages, profit and rent. *'Wages, profit, and rent, are the three original sources of all revenue as well as of all exchangeable value. All other revenue is ultimately derived from some one or other of these'.*

- Focus – target your offering to a niche group.

If you decide to target your product or service, you must also consider the first two points and decide whether you will compete on price or difference alone. Competing on price has made many people rich, but it requires economies of scale that few enjoy. It may be possible for Wal-Mart or Tesco to drive down supplier costs but not everyone has that sort of muscle. Therefore, it is wiser to compete through differentiation and focus.

Smith points out that not everyone making money is selling a product or service: there is also a very lucrative business in money. Interest is the compensation paid to the lender, *'for the profit which he has an opportunity of making by the use of the money'.* This additional ability to make money is at the heart of a capitalist, free market system. Those with money have always lent it to those who don't have it, but need it to take advantage of business opportunities. Over time, this process has created banks. Like them or loathe them, they are essential for the global economy.

Smith warns, however, *'The interest of money is always a derivative revenue which if not paid from the profit must be paid from some other source.'* He also advises that borrowing to pay off other debt is a recipe for disaster.

YOUR THOUGHTS

THE MARKET DICTATES PRICE

Trying to squash a rumour is like trying to unring a bell.
- SHANA ALEXANDER, Journalist

Smith is obviously an avid admirer of letting the market decide and certainly if everyone plays fair, it's a good system but people don't always play fair.

'Different accidents' are not always accidents. In late March 2008 rumours began to circulate that one of the UK's biggest banks – Halifax Bank of Scotland (HBOS) – was experiencing liquidity problems. Those rumours wiped more than £3 billion (or 20%) off the bank's market value in just one morning of trading as worried investors pulled out. This is known as 'trash and cash' and considering there's an actual term for this type of market manipulation, this would indicate that it's not an accident at all! Basically, traders can make a great deal of money by 'shorting stock' or betting that a share price will fall. It doesn't take a genius to work out that starting a rumour greatly assists that process. In an unprecedented move, the Financial Services Authority (FSA) issued a sharp warning about market abuse. However, in their subsequent Inquiry, they were rather unsurprisingly unable to uncover enough hard evidence that the rumour had been deliberately set in motion.

FOOD FOR THOUGHT
If you want to invest in the stock market, but don't have the time or inclination to work out which rumours are true and which ones are deliberate manipulations, consider investing in the Index, i.e. FTSE, Dow Jones or NASDAQ instead of investing in particular stocks of a company of your choice. Have a financial advisor explain how this works and why it is potentially safer than buying individual stock.

'Different accidents' can also take the form of what Nassim Nicholas Taleb terms, 'Black Swans' – totally random, unpredictable and extremely rare events. Taleb is a former quantitative analyst and derivatives trader who made $40 million from shorting the market on Black Monday in 1987. Today, he is the Dean's Professor in the Sciences of Uncertainty at the University of Massachusetts and is described as one of the world's most sought-after thinkers. He believes that most city traders are like children picking pennies off the road in front of a steamroller: in other words, the majority of those inside the industry have no idea what they are doing or the potential damage they can cause. As the title of his first book suggests, Taleb believes we are Fooled by Randomness (2007) and that the arrival of completely unpredictable 'different accidents' such as the events of 9/11 can cause catastrophic consequences that we have no way of predicting.

Smith reminds us that, 'whatever may be the obstacles which hinder [price] from settling in this centre of repose and continuance, they are constantly tending towards it'. This can be evidenced by the immediate aftermath of 9/11, when the Dow Jones Industrial Average declined by 14% and yet, in just over two months, recovered to pre-9/11 trading!

YOUR THOUGHTS

SECRETS ARE
GOOD FOR BUSINESS

Intellectual Property has the shelf life of a banana.
- BILL GATES, Microsoft Billionaire

Smith says that if it *'was commonly known their great profit would tempt so many new rivals to employ their stock in the same way, the effectual demand being fully supplied the market price would soon be reduced'*. If you find yourself in a business that is highly profitable either because there are few competitors or because you have some trade secret that gives you an advantage, it's simply shrewd business to keep that knowledge to yourself. Otherwise you risk stiffer competition or imitation and your advantage will be lost. That is why it's so important to protect your intellectual property and patent your inventions. Keeping competitive advantages close to your chest is sensible but for most businesses, realistically they can't be kept forever.

Unless, of course, you are Coca-Cola®! They have successfully preserved the secret formula invented by Dr John Pemberton in 1886. Although how much is true and how much is marketing spin is a little hard to quantify. Coca-Cola have tinkered with the recipe and even tried to improve it dramatically with the introduction of 'New Coke' in 1985. This caused a severe customer backlash and the company hasn't touched the recipe since. Coca-Cola stands as a profitable reminder of

---
FOOD FOR THOUGHT

If your marketing appears to be getting a little tired and isn't pulling in the same response as it used to, try adding the word 'secret' to your copy! Is there a way to re-package your product or service around the idea of scarcity to make it exclusive and available to only a select few? If so, test this against your existing marketing approach to see which draws the most response.

WORDS OF WISDOM

Adam Smith says that, 'When the market price of some particular commodity happens to rise a good deal above the natural price, those who employ their stocks in supplying that market are generally careful to conceal this change.' In other words, secrets are good for business because they keep prices artificially high.

the financial potential of secrets.

Post-it notes were not so lucky. Although the original still enjoys the kudos of being the first to market, the secret to their success is either out or has simply been replicated by thousands of imitators: evidence of Smith's statement that, 'Secrets of this kind, however, can seldom be long kept; and the extraordinary profit can last very little longer than they are kept.' However, he acknowledges that, 'Secrets in manufacturers are capable of being longer kept than secrets in trade.'

The reason is probably financial. It costs more to initiate a competitive challenge to an existing manufacturer because of the start-up or modification costs associated with manufacturing. This cost usually allows existing manufacturing to maintain an advantage for longer.

Smith goes on to suggest that, 'A monopoly granted either to an individual or to a trading company has the same effect as a secret'... As a result, 'The price of monopoly is upon every occasion the highest which can be squeezed out of the buyers.' So, secrets may be good for business, but they are rarely good for the customer!

YOUR THOUGHTS

CREATE A MONOPOLY

Like many businessmen of genius he learned that
free competition was wasteful, monopoly efficient. And so
he simply set about achieving that efficient monopoly.
- MARIO PUZO,
Author of The Godfather

The result of restrictive practices is that competition in a particular area is kept low to create, *'enlarged monopolies [that] may frequently, for ages together, and in whole classes of employment, keep up the market price of particular commodities above the natural price'*. In other words, price fixing!

The airline industry has been dogged with price-fixing scandals. In August 2007, in a joint investigation by the Office of Fair Trading and the US Department of Justice, British Airways was shamed as 'conspirator' and fined £270 million for its role in a price-fixing cartel. Virgin Atlantic avoided a fine after it exposed the scheme. Both BA and Virgin Atlantic also settled a £100 million class-action lawsuit brought on behalf of passengers angry at overcharges because of the cartel.

In November 2007 Qantas was fined $61 million in the US, while in October 2008 the airline was fined a further $20 million by the Australian Competition and Consumer Commission (ACCC). BA was also fined another $5 million by the ACCC. Although BA seems to be

---

FOOD FOR THOUGHT

Price fixing is illegal, but differentiating yourself so that you stand head and shoulders above the competition is not. If you want to stand out, consider guaranteeing your product or service with an extraordinary guarantee. This demonstrates that you have faith in your own business and can help potential customers over the line as it allows them to feel secure in their choice.

consistently involved in price-fixing scandals they are not alone. Japan Airlines and Korean Air Lines have also been charged for keeping the market price, 'above the natural price'.

One of the most infamous examples of price-fixing was uncovered with the collapse of Enron. Kenneth Lay wanted to create an 'Energy Bank'. Friends in high places, such as George W. Bush, helped make it possible. By the end of 2000 Enron controlled a quarter of the US natural gas business. In tapes made public in 2004, Enron traders can be heard asking the El Paso Electric Company to shut down production in order to manipulate the price. In just six months California experienced thirty-eight rolling blackouts no doubt caused by the same deliberate manipulation.

Smith warns us that, 'such enhancements of the market price may last as long as the regulation of police which give occasion to them'. Enron, for one, did get caught but it was much too late for many. By the time vice president Sherron Watkins blew the whistle on Enron, it was too late to save thousands of jobs and innocent investors. Money was siphoned off before the collapse and those involved went on to infect the entire financial system. Political lobbying or, as it should be called, legalised bribery still goes on, vested interests lead to corruption as surely as night follows day.

YOUR THOUGHTS

AVOID DIVISIVE
MANAGEMENT

A spoonful of honey will catch more flies
than a gallon of vinegar.
- BENJAMIN FRANKLIN,
one of America's founding fathers

The archetypal characters in this age-old play involve, on one side, the hard-done-by worker, who finds new and novel ways to waste time, laze around and actively sabotage the company's success. On the other side is the tyrannical businessman, who pays as little as possible, and sees his workforce as nothing more than cogs in a profit-making machine. And yet in truth neither is wholly true. There is good and bad on both sides, but modern business is discovering that the only way to prosper is to value the role everyone plays and reward good performance. Smith writes, 'it is in vain for [anyone] to expect [help and cooperation] from benevolence only. [An employer] will be more likely to prevail if he can interest their self-love in his favour, and show them that it is for their own advantage to do for him what he requires of them.'

Scores of management theories focus on reward for good effort rather than punishment for bad performance. One such theory – Open Book Management – was developed by Jack Stack of the Springfield

---

FOOD FOR THOUGHT

Investigate some of the profit sharing, collaborative management styles on offer and find one that could work for your business. It doesn't need to involve elaborate re-structures or expensive culture change consultants, start small, involve your people and see what happens. To encourage business improvements create an 'improvement fund' and offer a percentage of cost savings or a cash incentive to staff.

WORDS OF WISDOM

When discussing wages, Adam Smith points out, *'The workmen desire to get as much, the masters to give as little as possible.'* Unfortunately this division between employer and employee is as relevant today as it obviously was then. Stereotypes of 'them and us' still don't help anyone.

Remanufacturing Corporation (SRC) in the US: along with twelve other executives, Stack made a management buy-out of the business in an attempt to save the 119 jobs from certain redundancy. There wasn't time to restructure and so Stack, an avid sports fan, created The Great Game of Business to save the company. Essentially the business was set up like a game – everyone knew their position, they were familiar with the rules and everyone understood that they would share in the rewards of success and the consequences of failure. What he found was that when people were personally motivated, not only to keep their job but also to share in the financial success of their hard work, the business was radically transformed.

Creating an empowered workforce is not for the faint-hearted. It requires trust and courage, but the rewards can be significant. The award-winning US study, 'The impact of human resource management practice on turnover, productivity, and corporate financial performance', concluded businesses practising workplace empowerment are more profitable, generate more sales per employee and have less staff turnover.

Treating staff badly results in low morale, high staff turnover and escalating recruitment costs, so it's far better to join forces and offer a slice of the profit pie to employees who consistently deliver.

YOUR THOUGHTS

_____

_____

_____

_____

PAY YOUR PEOPLE WELL

There is one rule for industrialists and that is:
Make the best quality of goods possible at the lowest
cost possible, paying the highest wages possible.
- HENRY FORD,
Founder of the Ford Motor Company

'A man must always live by his work, and his wages must at least be sufficient to maintain him.' Eighteenth-century employers realised there was a point beyond which they could not reduce wages because the worker would no longer survive. Obviously if the workers were not paid enough to support themselves and bring at least four children into the world, of which two hopefully reached adulthood, who would be available to do all the work?

Henry Ford recognised this conundrum and in 1914 he increased pay in his automotive factories from $2.50 a day to $5.00. Ford was not exactly known for his belief in workers' rights and was by all accounts the stereotypical hard-nosed businessmen, so why did he decide to double employee wages? Pure entrepreneurial self-interest!

Ford recognised that recruitment costs were a significant expense in his business, mind-numbingly dull production line work takes its toll and staff turnover was high. Doubling wages helped appease that, if

---

FOOD FOR THOUGHT

If you are in business, don't assume your job is to drive down your wages bill. Instead, have your new employee suggest their own salary package on condition that they create a detailed description of what they will do for the business in the first six months together with measurable Key Performance Indicators. They will then need to live up to those promises.

at least temporarily. But most importantly, he recognised that if he was to create his dream car company, then he needed to expand the market beyond the elite. Cars needed to become affordable to the mass market so that owning a car was an aspiration and achievable dream for the average worker. The only way to do this was to pay his staff enough money so that they could afford to buy his product: the strategy worked.

Money needs to keep moving if it is to turn the cogs of business. If you cut costs in the supply side by bickering over wages, you may inadvertently limit your own demand. People need to be paid enough to allow them to spend what they earn and create a demand for products and services. It is this challenge that faces an economy in a downturn. Consumers panic and stop spending their money, causing the wheels of industry to grind to a halt, further exacerbating an already difficult situation.

Smith reminds us that, *'In order to bring up a family, the labour of the husband and wife together must, even in the lowest species of common labour, be able to earn something more than what is precisely necessary for their own maintenance.'* So, pay your people well and allow everyone to prosper.

YOUR THOUGHTS

DON'T HAVE CHILDREN!

Children are poor men's riches.
- JOHN RAY,
English Naturalist

Obviously *The Wealth of Nations* concerns the wealth of nations. Smith is uniquely occupied with what makes people, business and ultimately, countries wealthy. In his time, one way was to have kids. According to his calculations, 'The labour of each child, before it can leave their house, is computed to be worth a hundred pounds clear gain.'

According to a survey conducted by financial services provider Liverpool Victoria the average cost to parents of raising a child from birth to twenty-one years old is £180,137! Published in November 2006, the report states that the average UK household spends £17,002 on a child's food, £12,352 on clothing, £11,086 on holidays, £9,592 on hobbies and toys, and £5,518 on pocket money.

Education is a huge expense costing on average £46,778, even if the state system is used. If your child has aspirations of university, expect to pay an additional £12,153 per year. The cost of attending university now stands at £32,478, which includes tuition fees, books and living costs.

FOOD FOR THOUGHT

The idea of children working is not all bad. I was brought up on a working farm and expected to help during busy times. In exchange, pocket money was paid for chores. Not only did this help spread the load but it also taught me an important lesson: there's no such thing as a free lunch! If your child gets pocket money or wants extra for a special event or item, negotiate with them for what they are prepared to do or give in return.

Even assuming these figures have been warped by some very spoilt children and represent a mathematical average rather than the typical child, raising kids is still an expensive undertaking. Children may well be a source of joy, and hopefully pride, but rarely of opulence and prosperity – unless, of course, your offspring happens to star in Harry Potter! Based on these figures it's no wonder that a separate survey for the same company found that in almost two-thirds of UK families (61%), both parents have to work to cover the cost of raising a family.

In the eighteenth century, 'The value of the children is the greatest of all encouragements to marriage.' Rather amusingly, although not for the woman in question, Smith goes on to note that even poverty isn't an obstacle, 'A half-starved Highland woman frequently bears more than 20 children, while a pampered fine lady is often incapable of bearing any, and is generally exhausted by two or three.' 'Barrenness, so frequent among women of fashion, is very rare among those of inferior station.' I wonder what Smith would make of modern-day career woman? He does, however, concede that poverty isn't so great for the kids involved: 'The tender plant is produced, but in so cold a soil and so severe a climate, soon withers and dies.'

──────── YOUR THOUGHTS ────────

COLLABORATION IS BETTER
THAN DOMINATION

In the long history of humankind (and animal
kind, too) those who learned to collaborate and
improvise most effectively have prevailed.
- CHARLES DARWIN,
English Naturalist

This idea of collaboration is one that was taken further by French sociologist and philosopher Emile Durkheim. His theory of collective representation is the social power of ideas stemming from their development through the interaction of many minds. Durkheim is still considered one of the most influential figures in sociology and his commentary often acts as a counterbalance between Smith's capitalist ideals and Karl Marx's totally socialist vision.

Smith often seems at pains to infuse his argument with morality and ethics. Perhaps I'm being optimistically generous, but his earlier work on ethics, *The Theory of Moral Sentiment* (see also page 1), together with his subtle insistence that a collective, collaborative approach is always preferable to dominance and servitude, indicates a genuine belief in this philosophy. Perhaps he fully appreciated the failings and potential for exploitation that Durkheim was so keen to expose. A free market economy lends itself perfectly to manipulation by unscrupulous practitioners and perhaps Smith wanted to do his bit to veer people away from exploitation. However, he was also a canny Scot who

---
FOOD FOR THOUGHT

Could you become part of the free agent nation? Does your job have outsourcing possibilities, where you might collaborate with other employers and offer a better service for less time and more money? During economic difficulties it is always wise to assess your current skills and see where else they could be used and who else might be willing to pay for them.

> ——— WORDS OF WISDOM ———
>
> Smith concludes his discussion on labour by saying, *'The greater their numbers, the more they naturally divide themselves into different classes and subdivisions of employment. More heads are occupied in inventing the most proper machinery for executing the work of each, and it is therefore more likely to be invented.'*

understood that the only way to do so was to appeal to economic, rather than social sensibilities.

In addition, it was clear to Smith that, *'The superiority of the independent workman over those servants who are hired by the month or by the year and whose wages and maintenance are the same whether they do much or do little is likely to be still greater.'*

In modern times this idea can be seem unusual amid the growth in outsourcing. Daniel Pink wrote a book called *Free Agent Nation* (2002), in which he talks about the 'new movement' sweeping across America and beyond. According to Pink, up to twenty-five million independent 'free agents' in the US alone contracted their services out to employers on a pay-per-use basis. This works for the employer because they get to keep staff costs down and they can be assured of a high standard of work from the contractor, but it also suits the individual, who is able to charge more for his or her skills, gain autonomy and long-term security.

In business, there is an almost instinctive compulsion to keep labour costs to an absolute minimum and yet Smith points out that this strategy is not only counterproductive to long-term success, but if you don't look after your workforce and encourage their participation they will not create the innovations that could pave the way for even greater success.

——— YOUR THOUGHTS ———

DON'T READ THIS CHAPTER!

Forbidden things have a secret charm.
- PUBLIUS CORNELIUS TACITUS,
Senator and Historian of the Roman Empire

What's especially interesting about his statement is the psychology of it. Chances are that if you were flicking through this book and browsed down the contents page, this chapter title might have caught your interest – you may even have skipped forward to read it. Why is that?

So, why are we innately drawn toward things that are prohibited? I remember watching an episode of the TV programme *Trick or Treat*, where illusionist Derren Brown demonstrates all sorts of psychological tricks and perceptual manipulations. In one show, blue boarding with a little hole in it was placed along a relatively busy walkway. Above the hole was a sign that read, 'Do not look through this hole'. There was, of course, a secret camera filming what happened and countless people were unable to resist looking through the hole. Brown put this down to a combination of our rebellious urge to fight commands not to do something, plus curiosity.

In his groundbreaking book, *Influence, Science and Practice* (2000), Dr Robert B. Cialdini talks about the six basic principles of psychology

---
FOOD FOR THOUGHT

If you want to stop someone doing something, think twice about prohibiting it! Also, be aware of how easily marketers manipulate you. This is especially easy and cost-effective online, where marketers can very simply create the impression of a limited offer which looks as if it's about to expire, yet if you returned to the site you would notice the date had changed and it was about to expire again!

that direct human behaviour which may shed some light on this. The
work is the result of extensive experimental studies on what persuades
people to act. Social proof and scarcity are of particular interest here
and might go some way toward explaining why so many people looked
through the hole.

Social proof is when we are assured of a correct course of behaviour
not by instruction, but by watching to see what others do. In the TV
show certainly more people were tempted to have a look through
the hole when others were doing the same. In addition, the principle
of scarcity also plays a role. The fear that we might miss out on
something is also a driving force to action. This principle is used very
effectively by the marketing industry, which creates the illusion of
scarcity and taps into our innate fear of missing out. We are encouraged
to buy today because the offer is about to expire or because only a
limited number remains.

In many ways the reasons why are unimportant. What is important is
that if we are inherently curious about anything prohibited, surely this
raises some very serious questions about everything from how we
raise our kids to tackling serious issues such as drug abuse.

───────────── YOUR THOUGHTS ─────────────

MONEY MAKES MONEY

Money is the seed of money, and the
first guinea is sometimes more difficult
to acquire than the second million.
- JEAN-JACQUES ROUSSEAU,
Philosopher, Writer and Composer

Gaining access to funds has always been difficult for business. In order to access funds, a business must demonstrate a track record of successful trade, secure the loan against some fixed asset such as property and/or provide personal guarantors who will assume the risk. Even a successful business wishing to expand may struggle to secure lending under such conditions – and that was before the credit crunch began in mid 2007.

Yet business is the lifeblood of any economy. In an effort to address this serious funding challenge for growing and fledgling businesses, the UK Government introduced the Small Firms Loan Guarantee scheme in 1981. Since then it has provided much-needed funding for more than 88,000 businesses. The scheme, which sees the Government secure up to 75% of the loan with the lender, was comprehensively reviewed in 2005 following reports that the process was needlessly bureaucratic and complicated. Changes were made, but just how effective they will be in the face of global credit problems remains to be seen.

FOOD FOR THOUGHT

First, ask yourself if you really need whatever it is you are desperate for. If the answer is still yes, then bargain hunt. Search online and consider using sites like TrialPay (https://merchant.trialpay.com), where you can get what you need for free, provided you buy something else. Recently I needed some anti-virus software and could get this for free if I also bought some printer cartridges (which I needed, anyway).

If business does not have access to the capital required for normal operation, how can they possibly survive during difficult times? Without access to funds to help weather the storm many businesses will fold, leading to increased unemployment and thus making a bad situation far worse. According to that logic business must be supported through difficult times, not to make excessive profits but just to tick over so that jobs may be kept and the economy bounces back sooner rather than later.

The irony of money is eternal: those who have access to it don't need it while those who do, can't get access! At least not without paying through the nose for it.

Smith says, 'When the law does not enforce the performance of contracts, it puts all borrowers nearly upon the same footing with bankrupts or people of doubtful credit. The uncertainty of recovering the money makes the lender exact the same usurious interest which is usually required for bankrupts.'

Exacting usurious interest rates is not, however, confined to the back streets of housing estates where loan sharks rule with an iron fist. The banks themselves have made a great deal of money lending to subprime lenders. As the name suggests, subprime simply means lenders below the ideal lending criteria, who were then penalised for that fact through higher interest rates.

YOUR THOUGHTS

WORKING IS GOOD
FOR THE SOUL

*I don't think that work ever really
destroyed anybody. I think that lack of
work destroys them a hell of a lot more.*
- KATHARINE HEPBURN, Actress

In 1897 Emile Durkheim (see also page 37) observed the link between unemployment and suicide. Durkheim, the father of sociology and the man credited with making sociology a science, made a massive contribution to the field that was in many ways a direct challenge to Smith's capitalist vision as he sought to illustrate the social consequences of a free market economy.

Having a job is more than just about making money; it offers a psychological framework that provides more than just economic benefits. A job imposes a time structure, it involves contact and shared experiences outside the family, it provides individual and collective goals, plus opportunities for achievement and imposes status and social identity; it also enforces activity – all of which function as psychological supports.

Dr David Fryer, psychologist from Stirling University in Scotland, has spent years studying the psychological effects of unemployment and concludes there are many 'worryingly consistent findings'. His s tudies showed that up to 40% of unemployed people suffered psychological distress.

FOOD FOR THOUGHT
If you find yourself out of work, volunteer! This may not solve your financial problems but it could help you through a difficult time. Keeping active and part of the community is not only good for self-esteem and morale, but it's impressive to would-be employers and keeps you connected so you hear about any job opportunities that may arise.

The vast body of knowledge on the subject demonstrates beyond reasonable doubt that unemployment causes poor psychological health. Anxiety, depression, dissatisfaction, emotional strain, negative self-esteem, hopelessness regarding the future and other negative emotional states are all higher in the unemployed than in matched groups of employed workers. There is also evidence that physical health is adversely affected. However, this research does not extend to the intentionally unemployed, who happily live at the taxpayer's expense. No early mornings, no tedious commute and no self-esteem for the 'why bother?' brigade. In the UK today, there are families where no one has worked for three generations.

In April 2008 public services think tank Reform (www.reform.co.uk) concluded successive governments have created a welfare-dependent culture that is a terrible legacy. A staggering six million Britons now live in homes where no one has a job and benefits are a way of life. Of those it was revealed that 20,000 British households make more than £30,000 a year in state benefits. It's easy to see why the 'why bother?' attitude exists: it's all too easy.

Reform also pointed out that inequality in the tax system meant that those receiving benefits who then find work face punitive rates of taxation: for every extra £ earned, up to 90% of their benefit is lost. Clearly counter-productive, this penalises those who genuinely want to work.

YOUR THOUGHTS

HOW WAGES
ARE DETERMINED

The tougher the job, the greater the reward.
- GEORGE ALLEN,
US Politician

Unsurprisingly wages are higher in those jobs that are disagreeable. The one that springs to mind is the person who cleans up a crime or accident scene once the police have left. Known as CTS Decon (Crime and Trauma Scene Decontamination), this niche area of the cleaning industry is both booming and lucrative. The 'disagreeableness' of the profession combined with the relatively few people with the stomach for it means that it is well paid.

How easy and cheap it is to train someone to do the job also plays a role in the establishment of wages. Stacking shelves in a supermarket, for example, doesn't require much training and isn't exactly difficult, subsequently the pay won't be great. A veterinary surgeon, on the other hand, spends at least six years studying, and if you want 'Tiddles' to survive her brush with the Ford Laguna, you'll need to pay for that expertise. A vet's wages are therefore considerably higher than a supermarket shelf stacker.

For those not consistently employed, wages are also higher. A sheep shearer, for example, only works for part of the year and as such can

---

FOOD FOR THOUGHT

If you have kids, make sure they understand the five variables constituting wages and consider them in their career choice. Like products, wages follow simple rules of supply and demand. If someone provides a difficult service or one in which not everyone can succeed, or that requires considerable training and trust in execution, then they will naturally compete in a limited market and their wages will reflect that.

charge more for his services when they are needed. In modern times, self-employed people of all sorts fall into this category and must pitch their services low enough to win business yet high enough to sustain them through the lean months.

Wages also vary according to the likelihood of success in pursuing that career and the amount of trust that must be placed in the person doing the job once they have qualified. Not everyone who wants to become a doctor or lawyer, for example, will successfully finish the training and go on to practice. Once they do, however, we are required to trust their knowledge and expertise, and consequently we pay for the peace of mind that a genuine professional can bring. This part of wages is usually closely linked to the length of training required to pursue a particular career.

Smith ends by drawing attention to one unusual profession that still offers profit potential, 'The keeper of an inn or tavern, who is the master of his own house, and who is exposed to the brutality of every drunkard, exercises neither a very agreeable nor a very creditable business. But there is scarce any common trade in which a small stock yields so great a profit.'

YOUR THOUGHTS

SUCCESS IS USUALLY
DEPENDENT ON ABILITY

*No amount of ability is of the
slightest avail without honour.
- ANDREW CARNEGIE,
Industrialist and Philanthropist*

Today, people seem more interested in where you went to school than any ability or lack thereof. Progression up the greasy pole of commerce is more down to nepotism and 'old boy networks' than talent or genius. Nowhere has this been more devastatingly demonstrated than the City.

Michael Sharpe (a pseudonym given by the press to protect his identity) was managing director of one of the largest trading desks in London's Canary Wharf. In an anonymous interview regarding the impact of the City's rampant bonus culture, he revealed, 'I was never under the illusion that I was worth my bonus. Last year [2007] I got $2.3 million, small fry relative to some of my peers, who raked in up to $30 million. But the truth is that any fool could have made money in the market in the past few years. It was easy. You could be mediocre and make millions.'

According to the Centre of Economic and Business Research £7.5 billion was paid out in bonuses across the City in 2007. An estimated 5,000 'Sharpes' received seven figure annual bonuses, and some hedge

---
FOOD FOR THOUGHT

Mediocrity married to excessive wealth only ever existed in the finance sector and the current financial crisis will no doubt eliminate that, at least in the short term. Concentrate on excellence in your field and then at least if you do end up making serious money, you will not fall victim to hubris and may sleep soundly in the knowledge that you're worth it! Focus on improving your knowledge and skill base by learning and practice.

WORDS OF WISDOM

Smith says, *'To excel in any profession, in which but few arrive at mediocrity, is the most decisive mark of what is called genius or superior talents.'* In his world it wasn't possible to reach the top of your field without talent. Ability mattered, although it is questionable whether it still does.

---

fund managers regularly banked over £100 million a year.

Smith adds, *'The overweening conceit which the greater part of men have of their abilities is an ancient evil remarked by the philosophers and moralists of all ages.'* No doubt, Sharpe is one of the few in the City who didn't believe his own bull***t, but he is certainly rare.

Banking executives, traders and CEOs are never anything more than shepherds of shareholder investment, yet they reap entrepreneurial style rewards without risking any of their own capital. These self-proclaimed 'Masters of the Universe' are employees, nothing more, and have never deserved the outrageous remuneration they once enjoyed.

This is a sentiment shared by some surprising people. In April 2008 the Governor of the Bank of England, Mervyn King, attacked the City's bonus culture, adding that a 'decade of excessive risk-taking' paved the way for the financial crisis that began in mid-2007.

King also lamented the bonus culture for causing a brain drain from other parts of the economy. In the US the financial sector also became a powerful magnet for academic talent. In 1970, just 5% of Harvard Business School graduates went into finance. By 2007, a whopping 30% from this prestigious college expected their first job to be in finance, not business.

YOUR THOUGHTS

PLAYING THE LOTTERY IS NOT AN ECONOMIC STRATEGY

Money never made a fool of anybody:
it only shows them up.
- ELBERT HUBBARD,
Writer, Artist and Philosopher

Smith writes, 'The soberest people scarce look upon it as a folly to pay a small sum for the chance of gaining ten or twenty thousand pounds; though they know that even that small sum is perhaps twenty or thirty per cent more than the chance is worth.' In other words, smart people don't think of the Lottery as a legitimate use of their capital toward wealth creation.

Considering that 70% of adults play The National Lottery on a regular basis, one can only assume that there aren't many 'sober' people in the UK. According to organisers Camelot, sales of lottery related products total around £100 million a week! Apparently the total yearly sales of National Lottery products are greater than the combined annual sales of UK firms Coca-Cola®, Warburton Bread, Walkers Crisps, Hovis Bread, Cadbury Dairy Milk, Nescafé, Andrex, Lucozade, Kingsmill Bread and Robinson's Soft Drinks!

Most people would assume that any horse at odds of a 100:1 was a donkey and wouldn't warrant any serious consideration as the potential

---

FOOD FOR THOUGHT

Take a few moments to work out just how much you spend on lottery products each week and multiply that average out for a year. Does the figure surprise you? What else could you buy with that money? Consider halving the amount you spend and putting the savings in a piggy bank that can't be opened. Then you have at least one guaranteed windfall every year.

winner. Yet on the faintest whiff of hope millions of people pour their hard-earned cash into the Lottery, which by the organisers' own admission, has odds of up to 13,983,816:1! With the British Government making £24 for every £1 Camelot achieve in profit, no wonder Lottery tickets are considered by many to be the 'tax on stupidity'.

However, lotteries have been around a long time. Foolishness or eternal optimism, it's open to debate. The first signs trace back to the Han Dynasty (between 205 and 187 BC). In Europe, the Roman Empire held lotteries for amusement but it wasn't until 1434 that the Dutch created the first public lottery and this didn't reach the UK until 1566. Lottery funding has helped finance everything from the Great Wall of China to the Sydney Opera House.

On the up-side, £25 million is generated for good causes every week. According to Camelot, 'More than 300,000 individual awards have been made across the UK in the biggest programme of civic regeneration since the 19th Century – that is an average of 103 lottery grants for every single postcode district!' Smith concludes that, *'There is not, however, a more certain proposition in mathematics than that the more tickets you adventure upon, the more likely you are to be a loser.'*

YOUR THOUGHTS

HOW INSURED
ARE YOU REALLY?

For almost seventy years the life insurance
industry has been a smug sacred cow feeding
the public a steady line of sacred bull.
- RALPH NADER,
Attorney and Political Activist

Smith would probably turn in his grave if he could see how 'very moderate profits' of insurance companies ballooned in the centuries following his death. So too might the two other Scots credited with inventing the insurance industry, as we know it today.

Friends Robert Wallace and Alexander Webster were hard-drinking Church of Scotland ministers from Edinburgh, who were acutely aware of the harsh conditions that people in their parish lived under. They were particularly concerned about the vulnerability of widows and children of ministers, who received half the year's stipend in the year of the death, but not much else. Together with fellow mathematician Colin Maclaurin, they created the first true insurance fund. Scottish Widows, as the fund became known, is still a major force.

Today, insurance has a fairly poor reputation for charging escalating premiums, while at the same time creating complex policy documents that confuse and discourage claimants. Small print tucked away at the back of a long and dull document ensures most people never read it. Consequently when something goes wrong, they often receive an

---

FOOD FOR THOUGHT

Find all your insurance policy documents and read them. If you want to save time, start at the back and read forward. That way, you'll miss all the sales fluff and congratulatory praise for your wise decision and skip right to the facts. Pay particular attention to the small print and caveats under which your claim will not be paid. Is it worth it?

unpleasant surprise.

In August 2005 Hurricane Katrina tore into the city of New Orleans: winds reaching 140 miles per hour ripped houses from their foundations and a 9-metre storm surge breached 3 of the levees protecting New Orleans from Lake Pontchartrain and the mighty Mississippi. The result was total devastation. Only 5 homes out of 26,000 were not flooded, 1,836 people lost their lives and Katrina exposed the inadequacy of the insurance industry. The people of New Orleans were not 'thoughtless' or 'rash' – they had insurance. No fewer than 1.75 million claims were made, with estimated insurance costs of $41 billion. Needless to say, every scrap of small print was used to avoid paying as many claims as possible.

In his book *The Black Swan* (2007), Nassim Nicholas Taleb talks about the random events that underlie our life. He tells the story of a casino that spent hundreds of millions of dollars on gambling theory and high tech surveillance yet four of the greatest, or narrowly avoided losses fell outside their sophisticated 'insurance' system.

Perhaps paying for insurance was smart in Smith's day, but is it really possible to insure yourself against risk when all the real risk is totally unpredictable and standard insurance often not worth the paper it's written on?

——————————— YOUR THOUGHTS ———————————

A LITTLE EXTRA CAN
MAKE A BIG DIFFERENCE

First secure an independent income then practice virtue.
- GREEK PROVERB

Smith always writes from the perspective of the employer. Occasionally he makes a statement that implies that he has considered the position of the employee and does his part, albeit small, to encourage humanity in business. *The Wealth of Nations* is the capitalist manifesto and as such, it is hardly surprising that the 'masters' side is taken. He is, in effect, discussing under what conditions employers are best able to get the upper hand with their employees: *'Firstly the employments must be well known and long established; they must be in their natural state [i.e. under normal trading conditions]; they must be the sole or principal employment of those who occupy them.'*

In Smith's era having your staff work solely for you was beneficial because it limited their options and therefore made them more dependent and potentially more amenable to employer demands. Today this is probably still true to some extent, especially in a contracting market where people are scared. During the discussion, however, Smith inadvertently tells employees how they may gain more control. If all your income derives from one place, any changes in that industry or

---
FOOD FOR THOUGHT

Visit www.guru.com to search for projects in your field. Look for small jobs that you might complete in your spare time and bid to carry out the work. This is an excellent way to make extra cash to pay off any outstanding debt more quickly. Paying more than required on your mortgage, for example, could save you thousands in interest. And it could even be the launching pad for a new career. Be sure to seek legal and taxation advice before you start.

workplace can be unsettling and stressful. Conversely, having multiple streams of income can make an individual less vulnerable to the whims of employers.

An increasing number of people now work at more than one job. Often this is because fewer full-time positions are available and it's a policy that has worked well for the employer because it allows them to avoid certain contributions. However, perhaps it's time that employees viewed this differently and embraced the diversity. By spreading the risk of sole employment and attaining new skills you can become more secure in your own ability to earn a living, irrespective of the employer or economic environment.

Daniel Pink (see also page 38) found that the 'counterintuitive truth' was that those who ventured out on their own without a traditional job ended up feeling more secure about their future than they ever did with one! But you don't have to jump out of full-time employment without a safety net. There are many websites offering individuals and companies the opportunity to bid on projects listed in their field of work. Thousands of these are open to professionals in all areas of business, including marketing, design, law, programming, engineering, fashion, finance and consulting. So, test the water and supplement your income – who knows where it might lead?

——— YOUR THOUGHTS ———

THE IMPORTANCE
OF EDUCATION

Tell me and I'll forget; show me and I may
remember; involve me and I'll understand.
- CHINESE PROVERB

In the late eighteenth century apprenticeships were a form of protectionism. The Statute of Apprenticeship enacted that no person, 'should exercise any trade, craft or mystery at the time exercised in England, unless he had previously served to it an apprenticeship of seven years at least'. It was therefore impossible to enter a trade without doing an apprenticeship – a fact that kept supply for certain professions low, while prices remained high.

Smith recognised this was unjust considering, *'The patrimony of a poor man lies in the strength and dexterity of his hands; to hinder him from employing this strength and dexterity in whatever manner he thinks proper without injury to his neighbour is a plain violation of his most sacred property.'*

Interestingly, he raises the question and validity of long apprenticeships because he felt this hindered the free market and was therefore not in the best interests of the customer, who was effectively held to ransom by the limited number of people in any one industry. In addition, long apprenticeships actively stopped poorer people from

---

FOOD FOR THOUGHT

If you have kids, encourage them to consider all the options. Education doesn't just happen in a classroom; expand their thinking with non-fiction books. Encourage them to seek out opportunities, volunteer their time and gain some experience in business. Often working your way up, going travelling or volunteering overseas can differentiate an individual far more than the traditional route of higher education.

using their skills and industry to get ahead. Instead, Smith suggests, 'long apprenticeships are altogether unnecessary', stating that in many professions there isn't any great mystery if those familiar with it are willing to pass on their knowledge. The education required to become a specialist is not, therefore, down to time or education, but to the quality of that education.

Nothing much has changed. If you imagine for a moment that the figures on the cost of raising children (see also page 35) are remotely accurate, putting a child through university will set you back over £30,000. If you also consider that the average student graduates £14,161 in debt, then it's a questionable use of time and money. University can be great fun and broadens a young person's horizons, but it's not a guaranteed passage to success, especially when individuals are saddled with significant debt before they have even begun earning!

Perhaps it's time for bright kids just to go into the world of business, learn on the job and demonstrate their ability as Smith suggested. After all, 'They who are soonest in a condition to enjoy the sweets of [their labour] are likely soonest to conceive a relish for it, and to acquire the early habit of industry.'

—— YOUR THOUGHTS ——

FALLING STANDARDS
OF EDUCATION

My education was interrupted only by my schooling.
- WINSTON CHURCHILL,
Orator, Historian, War Leader
and British Prime Minister

Apparently holding the attention of pupils has been a problem for hundreds of years, not a new phenomenon at all. Interestingly, Smith lays the blame squarely at the teachers' feet, *'No discipline is ever requisite, no force attendance upon lectures which are really worth the attending.'* In other words, had the teacher enough of a grasp on the subject they were employed to teach, they would be able to bring that knowledge to life with modern examples and ideas to enthuse pupils and encourage learning. Instead, Smith suggests that incompetent teachers simply read from dusty old textbooks often written in a 'foreign and dead language'. Although to be fair, it can't be easy being an unappreciated teacher!

In modern times those lamenting the falling standards of teaching in the UK have pointed to the 11-plus and suggested today's children wouldn't be able to answer the questions. The 11-plus was established in 1944 to help the most able children from disadvantaged backgrounds reach their potential by qualifying them for state grammar schools with the emphasis on academic subjects. It was taken by all pupils at the end of

---

FOOD FOR THOUGHT

If you are helping your kids with their homework and you can actually help, try and make the subject relevant to them. Most people find it easier to understand something new when they can see the relevance of the idea in real life. If you can find ways of making abstract concepts come to life, your child (or anyone else for that matter) is much more likely to understand.

primary school and had the potential to change the entire course of a child's life. The question is, could an 11-year-old today divide 5,408 by 26, or figure out how many people were at the party when one-sixth of those present were adults, four-ninths were girls and the remaining 42 were boys – both questions from an 11-plus exam. But then again, could an 11-year-old from the 1950s master technological advances in the blink of an eye?

Smith's distress at the quality of teaching is mentioned several times in his books and is largely due to his belief in its vital importance. According to him there are four ways that naturally introduce subordination: 'The first is the superiority of personal qualifications, of strength, beauty, and agility of body; of wisdom and virtue, of prudence, justice, fortitude and moderations of mind… The qualifications of the mind can alone give very great authority.'

Considering the second is age, the third is wealth and the fourth is superiority at birth, i.e. royalty gaining an education, this is one of the few ways over which we have any control. Plastic surgery aside, there's not much that we can do about beauty, body or strength, so education is critical to progress in this world.

——— YOUR THOUGHTS ———

GENDER AND MONEY

Women's battle for financial equality has barely been
joined, much less won. Society still traditionally assigns
to woman the role of money-handler rather than
money-maker, and our assigned specialty is far more
likely to be home economics than financial economics.
- PAULA NELSON, Writer

It's obvious from the tone of *The Wealth of Nations* that it was written at a time when women didn't concern themselves with talk of finance. According to the men of the day, it would have been beyond them, anyway. For centuries, women have endured prejudice regarding their ability to manage money. Even as recently as the 1970s, they have been systematically rated less credit-worthy than men. Just how unjustified is the airhead, spendthrift stereotype can be demonstrated by the success of microfinance.

Microfinance was founded by Nobel Prize winner Professor Muhammad Yunus, who realised the potential of making small loans to women when studying poverty in his native Bangladesh. He founded the mutually owned Grameen ('Village') Bank in 1983. As of November 2008, Grameen Bank had 7.64 million borrowers, 97% of whom were women. With 2,536 branches, the bank provides services in 83,415 villages, covering more than 99% of the total villages in Bangladesh. Most of these loans are to women without any collateral. What they do have, however, is pride and determination. Since its inception Grameen

---

FOOD FOR THOUGHT

Give your kids a financial education and teach them the basics about money regardless of gender. Make sure they understand the devastating consequences of debt. It's far better for them (and for you) if they learn from an early age how to be financially prudent.

Bank has made microloans worth more than $3 billion and is perhaps one of the few banks in the world unscathed by the financial crisis of 2007/08.

Grameen Bank says they focus on women because they are often, 'neglected in society. Through the opportunity of self-employment and the access to money, Grameen Bank helps to empower those women. In addition, studies have shown that the overall output of development is greater when loans are given to women instead of men, as women are more likely to use their earnings to improve their living situations and to educate their children.'

From the slums of Bolivia to Nairobi to villages in India, the microfinance model has been taken up around the world. The money is often used to buy livestock or start micro businesses. What makes it work is the borrowers' genuine pride that comes from taking their financial destiny into their own hands. Not only does microfinance provide families with a way out of poverty, it does so while flying in the face of convention. According to traditional banking the poor are a bad credit risk, yet the loan default rate in microfinance is significantly lower than traditional banking!

Smith says, 'In every part of her life a woman feels some advantage from every part of her education.' If that education includes money management, then he is correct.

YOUR THOUGHTS

CHOOSING THE RIGHT PROFESSION

The harder the conflict, the more glorious the triumph.
What we obtain too cheaply, we esteem too lightly:
'Tis dearness only that gives everything its value.
- THOMAS PAINE,
English Revolutionary

His point is that the 'art of the farmer' and *'many inferior branches of country labour require much more skill and experience than the greater part of mechanic trades'.* This was due to those in the country, 'being accustomed to consider a greater variety of objects' and therefore their trade, *'is generally much superior to that of the other, whose whole attention from morning till night is commonly occupied in performing one or two very simple operations'.* (As a farmer's daughter I laughed when I read this and just had to include it.)

Throughout my life, I have always been hugely amused by the stereotypes I've met. If I had a pound for every time someone expected me to have straw in my teeth, I'd be a rich woman. My personal favourite was when the headmaster wrote on my university application form, 'She has a variety of interests, which despite coming from a farming background, are not all related to that area!' Ironically, I am now a writer (although I can lamb a sheep in an emergency), another profession that Smith targets. Apparently the Church got involved in education and it didn't work out well for the 'men of letters'.

FOOD FOR THOUGHT

If you are seeking a more satisfying career or you have kids about to embark on that journey, find out about Instinctive Drive™. This is a personality profiling tool that offers insight into what makes you tick so you can seek out professions that work with your innate nature rather than against it. It can be found at www.idcentral.com.au.

Smith suggests that these 'unprosperous' fellows could have enjoyed the same standing and compensation as lawyers and scientists, had the Church not paid for their education. The numbers taking up this 'free' education meant there was an oversupply of writers, which forced the price down. As a consequence, their options were limited and they usually ended up as teachers, another profession that still to this day doesn't enjoy the reverence it deserves.

So, what can be drawn from Smith's assertions about professions and the inequalities of both wages and kudos? First, they serve as a reminder not to jump to conclusions about someone's value or intelligence based on their professional choice. And ultimately, I believe Smith warns us against 'free' education. In today's world I would add 'easy' to that statement. If something is free or too easy, we don't value it – it's just human nature. That's why spoiling children is counter-productive to their long-term happiness. So, if you are sending your kids to university, make them contribute: encourage them to get a part-time job so they appreciate the real cost involved and work hard enough to make it matter.

YOUR THOUGHTS

THE CURSE OF CREDIT CARDS

*Nowadays people can be divided into three
classes – the haves, the have-nots and the
have-not-paid-for-what-they-haves.
- EARL WILSON, Politician*

John Biggins, an innovative banker at the Flatbush National Bank, New York, is responsible for our flexible friend. In 1947 he initiated a local community credit plan called 'Charg-It' that involved businesses located in two-square-blocks surrounding the bank.

The success of Biggins' idea attracted interest from other quarters. Two years later, Diners Club successfully launched their credit card. Within a year of inception Diners Club had managed to sign up 285 establishments and 35,000 cardholders, each paying $3 per annum for the privilege.

Today, the credit card business is enormous. In less than seventy years there has been an explosion in cards, allowing consumers easy access to money they have not earned. The consequences are nothing short of disastrous. According to Credit Action figures for December 2008, 27.4 million plastic card transactions will be made today with a total value of £1.56 billion. The total credit card debt in the UK for October 2008 was £53.1 billion, while the UK collective credit limit is £158 billion! The average interest rate on credit card lending is a whopping 17.9%,

---

FOOD FOR THOUGHT

Do not buy what you can't afford, do not buy what you can't afford, do not buy what you can't afford... Ask yourself, 'If I had to hand over cash for the item I'm about to purchase, would I still want it or be able to do so?' If the answer's 'No', don't buy it! I repeat, do not buy what you can't afford, do not buy what you can't afford...

which at the time of writing was a staggering 14.9% above the Bank of England base rate.

According to uSwitch 7.3 million customers withdraw $3.7 billion in cash each year from their credit cards with an average interest rate of 29.97%. This money is used by an estimated one million to pay mortgage, loan repayments and household bills. Over 200 years ago, Smith warned of these 'spendthrift' practices when he advised not to, 'contract a second debt in order to pay the interest of the first'.

The British Bankers' Association (BBA) reported the number of credit card balances bearing interest in September 2008 was a massive 73.2%. This means that almost three-quarters of all credit card users don't pay off the balance each month – which is the only sensible way to use them. Even those involved in the business know how financially ruinous credit debt can be. In 2003, Barclays' then chief executive Matt Barrett gave evidence at the UK Commons' Treasury select committee investigating credit card charges. He revealed, 'I do not borrow on credit cards. It is too expensive. I have four young children; I give them advice not to pile up debts on their credit cards.'

It's still wise to spend only what's derived from our labour.

--- YOUR THOUGHTS ---

SAFE AS HOUSES

Few rich men own their own property.
Their property owns them.
- ROBERT GREEN INGERSOLL,
Politician

The 'improvement of land' or 'fixed capitals' way of making money that spawned a love affair with property, created a series of booms and busts to rival any in the stock market. Until the middle of the twentieth century, home ownership was the domain of the wealthy.

The English-speaking obsession with property came out of Detroit, USA. Hub of the motor industry, Detroit was hit hard by the Depression that began at the end of 1929. In riots outside the Ford motor plant, five people were gunned down and anti-corporate sentiment ran high. President Franklin D. Roosevelt pioneered the idea of a property-owning democracy in a bid to pacify his people. It worked, and in the UK, too, home ownership flourished. Today there are around seventeen million owner-occupiers in Britain.

The surge toward home ownership in the English-speaking world meant a growing demand for mortgages, but the banks only had so much in deposits. Not to worry: in 1983 chief mortgage trader Lewis Ranieri at Solomon Brothers in New York came up with the idea of Collateralised

---

FOOD FOR THOUGHT

When you're buying a home, don't assume that interest rates will remain as they are. In the not-too distant past the base rate has been as high as 15%. Individual banks were charging even higher! Could you afford the house you want to buy if interest rates reached double digits? Make sure you can comfortably afford a reasonable rise in interest rates. Peace of mind is always more important than that extra bedroom!

Mortgage Obligations (CDO). Mortgages were no longer held by the bank, but bundled together and sold to investment funds eager for a little extra interest. This allowed banks to lend indefinitely.

Singly, the idea wasn't disastrous because mortgages were only given to those who could genuinely afford to repay them, but then George W. Bush signed the Dream Downpayment Act of 2003 saying, 'We want everybody in America to own their own home.' What followed was an avalanche of sub-prime loans. Ninja Lending had arrived (No Income, No Job or Assets!). CDOs were still used to re-fund banks only now they were toxic, backed by mortgages from people with no means or inclination of paying the mortgage once the low introductory interest rate ended.

The model worked beautifully when rates were low and property prices rose, but then the bottom fell out of the market: the underlying asset supposed to protect the bank was not worth what the borrower had paid for it. Throughout the US, 'Jingle mail' could be heard as occupiers moved out and mailed the keys back to the bank. Ironically, history repeated itself as the bad loans started to default in Detroit following a continuous downturn in the automotive industry. Sub-prime dominoes began to topple in the city where it all began, some eighty years before.

YOUR THOUGHTS

KEEP THE MONEY MOVING

Never invest in any idea you
can't illustrate with a crayon.
- WARREN BUFFET,
Billionaire Investor

Smith recognised the crucial role that trust plays in any economic system and, as we've witnessed, if you remove the confidence then the economic wheels of industry seize up. The first UK scalp from the US sub-prime problem was Northern Rock. Essentially, because the banks were lending mortgages, re-packaging the debt and selling it on to third parties, there was constant circulation or 're-capitalisation' of money back into the banking system. But then it all changed.

As home loans started to default in the US, the ratings agencies responsible for assessing risk on these complex investments realised that they had got it wrong, sending shockwaves through the financial markets. Banks, pension funds and investment houses became aware that some of their previously assumed supersafe Triple-A rated investments were not so! As a result, the banks quietly closed their doors and stopped lending as they tried to work out their exposure.

In September 2007, unable to re-capitalise on the inter-bank lending market, Northern Rock sought emergency funding from the Bank of England and sparked a 'run' as worried savers withdraw £2 billion within

---

FOOD FOR THOUGHT

The financial crisis that started in 2007 is perhaps the result of over-complication of the finance industry. Pointy-headed boffins have created complex financial instruments that few actually understand. Making shrewd investments is essential for financial prosperity, but only if you fully understand the upside and the downside. If you want to play the markets, make sure you understand them and can live with the worst-case scenario.

days. It was only when the UK Government stepped in to guarantee savings that trust was restored.

Since then the financial landscape has been decimated. Financial monoliths, such as Lehman Brothers and Merrill Lynch, disappeared from Wall Street. High Street banks on both sides of the Atlantic have been partially privatised to save them from collapse. 'Write-downs' by banks wiped at least $318 billion from banking balance sheets. In April 2008, the International Monetary Fund (IMF) estimated the sub-prime mortgage collapse is going to cost the world economy a staggering $945 billion! Icelandic bank Landsbanki collapsed, leaving 300,000 customers wondering if they would ever see their collective £5 billion again. As Niall Ferguson wrote in his book The Ascent of Money (2008), 'The subprime butterfly had flapped its wings and triggered a global hurricane.'

In late 2008, UK interest base rates were at a fifty-seven year low, but the London Inter Bank Offered Rates (LIBOR) was significantly higher. As a result, banks were still unwilling to lend to each other or customers, thus perpetuating the credit crunch which was pushing the economy into recession.

Smith reminds us, 'It obliges all [banks] to be more circumspect in their conduct, and not extending their currency beyond its due proportion to their cash.' Good advice that modern banking could do well to re-familiarise itself with.

———————— YOUR THOUGHTS ————————

KEEP THE COFFERS FULL

If it's too good to be true, it probably is.
- PLATITUDE

When the medium of exchange settled on money in the form of gold and silver coins it wasn't long before banks started issuing promissory notes instead of actual coins. Banks significantly increased the amount of money in the system by substituting coins for pieces of paper with no intrinsic value. These are the bank notes we know today. Smith reminds us, however, that the banks had expenses and obligations because of this system. First, they had to actually hold the equivalent gold and silver to the promissory notes issued, thus losing them potential interest, plus they had an obligation to replenish those stocks.

Banks have obviously been incredibly good at creating money out of thin air for many hundreds of years. Since Smith's time, government has conspired with banking to deregulate an industry, allowing 'financial weapons of mass destruction' such as Collateralised Debt Obligation (CDOs) and derivatives to emerge. Repacking debt and selling it on meant that the banks could profit indefinitely from interest payments.

On the other side, increasingly complex financial instruments were used to replenish money through investment, the most common and

---

FOOD FOR THOUGHT

It can be seen that having little in your coffers can be catastrophic for banking and the wider economy. The same is true of individuals. If you haven't already done so, set up an automated savings programme where 10% of your salary is diverted to a separate savings account. Do not touch that money under any circumstances and soon it will offer you a buffer and a little peace of mind.

potentially lethal of those being Options. These allow you to control shares at a fraction of the cost of actually owning them. Say, for example, you buy a Call Option that gives you the right, but not the obligation to buy shares for an agreed price at a certain time in the future. The cost of doing so is limited to the cost of the options contract, but if you are correct and the shares go up beyond the agreed price then you would exercise your right to buy the shares, knowing the market value is already higher. Theoretically this means you can make a killing while minimising your risk. If, however, you were the 'writer' or seller of that same Call Option and didn't already own the underlying stock, then you would have to buy the shares on the open market for a higher price than you sell them for, potentially losing millions in the process!

Smith warns of the 'Daedalian wings of paper money'. Today, complex financial instruments move invisible money around a vast financial labyrinth in a heartbeat. And yet Smith warns that coffers, 'empty much faster than if their business was confined within more reasonable bounds'. Clearly, bank de-regulation needs to be tempered with common sense and shareholders must come second to a dependable financial system.

— YOUR THOUGHTS —

THE PERILS OF INFLATION

*Inflation is when you pay fifteen dollars for
the ten-dollar haircut you used to get for
five dollars when you had hair.*
- SAM EWING, Writer

When Margaret Thatcher became Prime Minister in May 1979, the UK was struggling under double-digit inflation. Smith would probably have liked the 'Iron Lady' as she set about reinventing the economy using his free market principles. One tactic was to increase home ownership in the UK. Mortgage tax relief offered that incentive and tenants in council houses were given the option to buy their homes at rock bottom prices. The idea was simple – if you give people the opportunity to own a stake in the country through property, they will be more inclined to: (a) look after it and (b) work hard to protect it. The free market would encourage entrepreneurial activity and the economy would prosper.

The only real purpose of money is that it allows you to buy the things you need. Yet if inflation is allowed to escalate unchecked, the value or usefulness of that money falls. In the late 1980s, owner-occupier home ownership soared from 54% in 1981 to 67% just ten years later. Unfortunately, so too had interest rates, topping 15% in 1989! The same government that made home ownership possible was also

---

FOOD FOR THOUGHT

When times are good, often people don't care for bargain hunting, preferring to spend without any discernment. However, that soon changes when inflation eats away at the purchasing power of your pound. If inflation is high, try shopping at discount outlets – if you hunt for bargains, then you can frequently find a similar quality at a fraction of the big brand price.

WORDS OF WISDOM

Smith talks about inflation, *'Though we express a person's revenue by the metal pieces which are annually paid to him, it is because the amount of those pieces regulates the extent of his power of purchasing, or the value of the goods which he can annually afford to consume.'* He refers to the idea of inflation many times in *The Wealth of Nations*, but he never calls it that as such. Inflation is important because it affects the cost of living.

---

determined to rein in inflation. Raising interest rates doesn't only depress homeowners; it also depresses spending and therefore lowers inflation. The net effect was one of the most spectacular booms and busts in the history of the property market.

In addition, selling off council houses caused a serious shortfall in social housing because no new homes were built to take their place. Perhaps housing should be added to the list in Chapter 9 (see also page 20) – where food, water and shelter should never be left in the hands of capitalism.

The trouble with economics is that it's a balancing act. On the one hand, people need to spend to circulate capital and allow business to thrive. Conversely, too much circulation increases prices, and rising inflation means the money doesn't go so far. Smith reminds us that, *'Money is neither a material to work upon, nor a tool to work with; and though the wages of the workman are commonly paid to him in money, his real revenue consists not in the money, but in the money's worth; not in the metal pieces, but in what can be got for them.'*

YOUR THOUGHTS

_____

_____

_____

_____

ECONOMIES PROSPER
BY 'PRODUCTIVE LABOUR'

*Just as there is a trend toward high tech
today, there is another trend toward high
touch – homemade and wholesome.*
- MERYL GARDNER,
Marketing Specialist

Smith uses the examples of manufacturing and a 'menial servant' to illustrate his point about productive versus unproductive labour: *'The labour of a manufacturer adds, generally to the value of the materials which he works upon, that of his own maintenance and of his master's profit. The labour of a menial servant on the contrary adds to the value of nothing.'* His point is not that the menial service isn't of value, but that it cannot be stored and doesn't add value to the economy. In Smith's time the wealthy had servants and while their employers may have 'valued' their assistance around their stately home, they did not add to their wealth. If anything, they detracted from it. The factory owner, however, employing productive labour became wealthier as a result of that labour.

Smith equates this idea to governments and 'sovereigns', where the vast bulk of their expense is paid out on unproductive labour. Today, just check out your nearest roadworks to see the stark difference between productive private sector labour and unproductive public sector labour!

FOOD FOR THOUGHT

Making stuff is good for the soul and doesn't have to be done in a factory, so bring the idea of manufacture into your home. Start making things yourself instead of buying them – no one is too busy to grate cheese! Instead of buying a frozen lasagne that tastes of cardboard, hop online, print out a recipe and make it yourself! It's better for you, often cheaper and tastes a whole lot better.

WORDS OF WISDOM

Adam Smith writes about the accumulation of capital via labour and states, '*There is one sort of labour which adds to the value of the subject upon which it is bestowed: there is another which has no such effect. The former as it produces a value, may be called productive; the latter, unproductive labour.*'

Most likely, you will witness a dozen men standing around in bright yellow vests, leaning on shovels and looking down a hole that one of them made three weeks ago!

Smith reminds us that, '*A man grows rich by employing a multitude of manufacturers; he grows poor by maintaining a multitude of menial servants.*' If this is true of an individual, then it is also true of a community and a country. When you think of great manufacturing nations, Japan or China immediately spring to mind. China is booming largely because of their manufacturing based economy. This is no coincidence: most Chinese workers are employed in productive labour. That's no longer true of the UK, where only 14% of the total workforce is employed in manufacturing.

This must have consequences for the UK economy. In October 2008, the Office of National Statistics reported that UK manufacturing output fell by 4.9% compared to the same time in the previous year, the biggest drop in six years. A national aversion to making things may also be seen in the supermarket, where everything from grated cheese to frozen sliced lemon can be purchased. Are we really so inept or lazy that we buy frozen sliced lemon? Perhaps it's time to take note of Smith's advice and turn our attention back to productive labour.

YOUR THOUGHTS

THRIFT IS NOT
A DIRTY WORD

Wealth can only be accumulated by the earnings
of industry and the savings of frugality.
- JOHN TYLER, Tenth US President

A Banking innovation with serious consequences was 'home equity' – the difference between the current value of a property and the outstanding balance on a mortgage. As house prices rose, this created 'accidental millionaires' and billions were made available to eager homeowners keen to cash in on their appreciating asset. Only by 'drawing down' cash from their Home Equity Loan (HEL), they effectively handed their asset back to the bank through escalating debt. Because the bank held the asset as security, they didn't much care what people spent their money on. While some used the cash to add value to the asset, many did not. Their HEL may have allowed homeowners that holiday of a lifetime but the consequence was financial purgatory. Security in later life was replaced with mortgage obligations stretching way past retirement when the ability to meet those obligations would cease.

Based on current economic statistics, it's not just the word that is old-fashioned: parsimony implies financial thrift and care – concepts that seem alien to Western societies. According to the Office of National

---

FOOD FOR THOUGHT

According to the Yorkshire Building Society, the average Briton's savings would only last fifty-two days if they were unable to work. A staggering 36% would last eleven days! Work out just how long your current savings would last if you were unable to work. If the figure scares you, then do something about it. Cut back on unnecessary spending and try to increase your income.

Statistics, UK households saved just 1.1% of their income in the first quarter of 2008, the lowest figure since 1959. A faltering economy and high inflation certainly contributed to the sharp fall in savings. In the US, figures demonstrate that, starting in 2005, households have consistently spent more than they make for the first time since 1933.

An aversion to saving is not shared in China, however, where employees regularly save up to half their salary. This has led to significant Chinese investment in US Treasury bonds, resulting in China's 'nuclear option'. At the time of writing, China owns over $400 billion (or over 20% of the US debt), leaving America increasingly vulnerable to financial warfare, a political tactic that America is more than familiar with.

In 1956, US allies UK and France were engaged in battle against Egypt over control of the Suez Canal. Meanwhile, Russia threatened to intervene on Egypt's side. Desperate to avoid military action, the US requested the Allies withdraw. When they refused, the US – who at the time owned much of the UK debt – threatened to cut Britain's credit supply. Within weeks, all UK and French military forces withdrew from the region. Similarly, China now has the US by the financial short and curlies with 'nuclear'-sized consequences.

——————————— YOUR THOUGHTS ———————————

CONFINE YOUR EXPENSES
WITHIN YOUR INCOME

I am for a government rigorously frugal and simple;
applying all the possible savings of the public revenue
to the discharge of the national debt; and not for
increasing, by every device, the public debt, on the
principle of its being a public blessing.
- THOMAS JEFFERSON, Third US President

According to Kent Conrad, chairman of the Senate Budget Committee, it took 42 Presidents 224 years to run up $1 trillion of debt held abroad and yet George W. Bush has more than doubled this in seven years! America's founding fathers must be spinning in their graves. They were terrified by the national debt of $75 million following the War of Independence (1775–1783). It took forty-six years to pay off that debt, and in comparison to today's federal debt, this is pocket money!

Not all Presidents have practised financial mismanagement on the scale of Bush; some even tried to warn against exploitation of natural resources and overspending, but paid the ultimate political price. President Jimmy Carter made no fewer than four televised speeches in which he questioned America's rampant materialism, suggesting, 'Human identity is no longer defined by what one does, but by what one owns.' Carter was keen for his people to understand that the US was not the limitless land of plenty. His candour cost him the election. Americans didn't want to know about frugality and dwindling resources, they preferred the fairytale version perpetuated ironically

---
FOOD FOR THOUGHT
For one week, make a list of everything you spend, down to the last £1. Although tedious, this is usually highly illuminating – most people simply don't have a clue where their money goes. Make changes to pay off debt more quickly.

enough by an ex-Hollywood actor. On 20 January 1981, Ronald Reagan swept to power and with him came an explosion of federal debt during the 1980s.

The story's not much better in the UK. At the end of October 2008, the Public Sector Net Debt (PSND) was a colossal £640.9 billion. Interest for October alone was an eye-watering £3.39 billion. Granted, government intervention was necessary to help stave off a depression, but the big question is, why didn't the UK have a government surplus (savings) following over a decade of growth and prosperity? Like the US, the UK faces a financial time bomb that could prove catastrophic for future generations.

Smith states that, 'Great nations are never impoverished by private, though they sometimes are by public prodigality and misconduct.' Historians believe that the Roman Empire fell because of declining moral values, overextended and overconfident military overseas and fiscal irresponsibility by central government. On that basis, both the UK and US should be nervous as financial irresponsibility completes that trifecta. Both governments have acted like spendthrift parents, racking up huge debts that they expect their children to settle. With no frugality in office on either side of the Atlantic, for generations to come, taxpayers will pay a heavy price.

YOUR THOUGHTS

BANKRUPTCY IS NO LONGER A CALAMITY

Interest works night and day in fair weather and in foul.
It gnaws at a man's substance with invisible teeth.
- HENRY WARD BEECHER, Social Reformer

In Smith's day, people obviously went to great lengths to avoid bankruptcy or declaring insolvencies. Nowadays legislation appears to go to great lengths to make this extremely easy. According to the Insolvency Service there were 27,087 individual insolvencies in England and Wales in the third quarter of 2008. That's 298 people a day, or 1 every 4.8 minutes! This was an increase of 8.8% on the previous quarter and an increase of 4.6% on the same period in 2007. International accounting and consultancy firm KPMG predicts that number will rise to 150,000 in 2009, no doubt facilitated by further loosening of legislation, which makes bankruptcy even easier.

In 2009, Debt Relief Orders will allow low-income borrowers to declare themselves bankrupt online without attending bankruptcy court or dealing with the usual hassles and associated costs. However, it would be unfair to lump everyone in the same category. For some, it is simply the case that a business venture has gone wrong and certainly, there is something nobler about business related insolvency than credit card irresponsibility. Many famous entrepreneurs, including H. J. Heinz,

---

FOOD FOR THOUGHT

If you find yourself in financial difficulties, seek advice from an independent source such as the Citizen's Advice Bureau or similar organisations worldwide. If you go to a loan consolidation company, then they will advise you to do what's profitable for them, not necessarily the best for you. Consolidating loans simply means that you spread the payment terms out over a longer period and pay back even more interest than necessary.

WORDS OF WISDOM

According to Adam Smith, 'Bankruptcy is perhaps the greatest and most humiliating calamity which can befall an innocent man. The greater part of men, therefore, are sufficiently careful to avoid it.' Alas, in the twenty-first century many no longer seek to avoid it and see no stigma at all in bankruptcy.

Walt Disney and Milton Hershey of the chocolate empire, experienced bankruptcy before they made their fortune.

It is this fundamental desire to support industry that has created an even worse situation in the US. Born from the spirit of enterprise, the American Constitution supports that 'have a go' mentality without wishing to penalise too heavily when things go wrong, with repercussions. In America, between one and two million bankruptcies occur every year!

Meanwhile, in the UK, bankruptcy has at least some consequences. There are still certain professions from which you would be excluded, although bizarrely you would still be allowed to manage other people's money in the financial services industry or become an MP. In addition, you would almost certainly find access to credit severely limited. However, if you consider that the era of easy money is undoubtedly over, fewer people are gaining access to credit anyway, so it's questionable just how much of a difference being declared bankrupt will really make.

For those for whom personal responsibility is no foreign concept, an Individual Voluntary Agreement (IVA) may be a more preferable route. These are more flexible and allow the debtor to write off part of the debt while negotiating with creditors to repay the rest over an agreed timeframe.

YOUR THOUGHTS

_____

_____

_____

_____

INSTANT GRATIFICATION
IS EXPENSIVE

One man's trash is another man's treasure
- PROVERB

Like the idea of productive versus unproductive labour, money consumed immediately on indulgences does not add to wealth. The indulgences that Smith referred to were, 'a sumptuous table' and many servants. In modern times this could mean an overseas holiday that you couldn't really afford, or another few inches on that flat-screen TV.

Spending money on assets, on the other hand, adds to your overall wealth. Smith makes the point that the expensive assets of the rich soon find their way into the hands of others as the wealthy become bored and sell them off, thus offering the not-so flush the opportunity to purchase items that would previously be out of reach. Apparently, 'The marriage-bed of James the First was the ornament at an alehouse at Dunfermline.'

Today, we have eBay, a global marketplace that allows you to buy anything from a Vespa to a piece of toast with the grilled cheese depictions of the Virgin Mary! In 2004, the said piece of ten-year-old toast sold on eBay for $28,000. Although considering the cost and age of the item,

---

FOOD FOR THOUGHT

According to a survey conducted by ACNielsen International Research, more than 724,000 Americans use eBay as their primary or secondary source of income. In the UK, the figure is estimated to be in excess of 178,000. So, instead of hoarding stuff up in your attic that you never use, stick it on eBay and make some money from it! Recycle and repair items instead of buying new all the time. It's better for the environment and adds a little extra cash to your pocket.

> ### WORDS OF WISDOM
>
> Adam Smith writes about what type of expense contributes most to wealth: *'The revenue of an individual may be spent either in things which are consumed immediately, or it can be spent on things more durable, which can therefore be accumulated'*. Those immediately consumed are expensive to long-term wealth creation.

it was probably not 'consumed immediately'. Certainly, the Lord (and cheese) moves in mysterious ways!

eBay was created in 1995 by Pierre Omidyar, an avid internet enthusiast, who created an auction site to help his new wife find Pez™ dispensers to add to her collection! To test his invention, he offered a broken laser pointer, which sold for $14.83. Surprised, Omidyar contacted the winning bidder to ensure he realised the item was broken. The buyer answered, 'I'm a collector of broken laser pointers.' In that moment, Omidyar knew he was on to something.

He was right! eBay now has a global presence in 39 markets, helping 233 million registered users buy just about anything. Apparently a woman's handbag sells every three seconds, while former UK Prime Minister Lady Thatcher's handbag sold for £103,000! The most expensive item ever sold was a Gulf Stream Jet for a cool $4.9 million. In 2007, the value of sold items on eBay was almost $60 billion.

Smith reminds us that, *'The expense too, which is laid out in durable commodities is favourable, not only to accumulation, but to frugality.'* In other words, if you are sensible about your purchases and buy durable items that will retain some value, then if things become financially sticky you can always sell them without anyone ever knowing!

YOUR THOUGHTS

TAKE AN INTEREST
IN YOUR INTEREST

Man was lost if he went to a usurer, for the
interest ran faster than a tiger upon him.
- PEARL S. BUCK, Writer

In Smith's time, the law tried to prevent usury by fixing the highest rate of interest allowed without penalty. Today, usury is commonplace, not just by those sporting a menacing stare and a baseball bat! Pinstripe suits and corporate respectability are also in on the act.

At one end of the social spectrum you have people like Gerard Law, No. 1 loan shark in the deprived Hillington district of Glasgow for twenty years. In return for a loan, borrowers would hand over their benefit books. When the benefits were due, Law would give the borrower his or her benefit book back and collect his interest when they collected their money. The standard rate of interest was 25% per week, which works out at 11,000,000% a year! Needless to say, once you are in debt to a loan shark it's virtually impossible to escape. Eventually Law was jailed for ten months for his actions, but you can bet that as he left there were ten more men to take his place.

The problem is that loan sharks exist because of Smith's simple theory of supply and demand. There is a demand for money but no legitimate supply for the demographic most at risk. And that, according to the companies involved, is why mainstream lending is making its mark in

---

FOOD FOR THOUGHT

Credit cards aren't cheap! Do you know what rate of interest you are currently paying? Find all the documentation for your credit and store cards to discover exactly what Annual Percentage Rate (APR) you are paying. Cut up the card with the most extravagant interest rate and resolve to clear that debt first.

WORDS OF WISDOM

Adam Smith states, 'The man who borrows in order to spend will soon be ruined, and he who lends to him will generally have occasion to repent of his folly. To borrow or to lend for such a purpose, where gross usury is out of the question, [is] contrary to the interests of both parties.'

traditionally loan shark territory.

In 2004 the Competition Commission started an investigation into doorstep lending, following a super complaint by the National Consumer Council. The concern was that doorstep lending worth an estimated £2 billion a year targets the UK's poorest communities. It was the Commission's task to consider whether lenders were exploiting vulnerability and low levels of financial literacy to generate excessive profits. Despite average interest rates of 177%, with some even in excess of 1000%, the Commission discovered that in the absence of any other viable option most borrowers didn't care about the interest rates or cost of credit, only whether they could get hold of the money and afford the repayments.

The Commission found that, 'Profits substantially in excess of the typical cost of capital have been persistently earned by firms that represent a substantial part of the market.' However, they also discovered that most customers were satisfied with the services they received... hardly surprising, considering their options are extremely limited.

YOUR THOUGHTS

THE CONNECTION BETWEEN
PROPERTY AND INTEREST

I figure if I have my health, can pay the rent
and I have my friends, I call it 'content'.
- LAUREN BACALL, Actress

Easy credit, home equity and a booming property market led to the creation of the buy-to-let sector. For many, ambitions grew way beyond owning their own home; instead they saw property as an easy way to build wealth, especially as banks were falling over themselves to lend money. Northern Rock, the first bank to suffer from the US sub-prime fall-out (see also page 67) was also heavily involved in sub-prime lending in the UK. Offering 125% loans, not only had borrowers no need to demonstrate any financial prudence in saving for a deposit, but they would also receive a windfall cash bonus once they bought their home!

With money so freely available, why stop at just one property when you could own half a dozen and rent them out? The tenant would then be paying your mortgage while giving you a residual income on top. Fabulous!

This euphoria fuelled another industry: property investment seminars! Self-professed gurus cashed in on the frenzy of property ownership. I remember being asked to ghost a book for one such guru in Australia, who was charging $50,000 for some of his courses. At the time, banks

---

FOOD FOR THOUGHT

Try negotiating a long-term lease. In France far fewer people buy property and tenants have more rights. It's possible this sort of arrangement will cross the channel. If you have found a place you enjoy living in, then approach the owner to see if they would be interested in letting the property to you for an extended period of time so you have greater security.

WORDS OF WISDOM

Adam Smith states, 'The ordinary market price of land depends everywhere upon the ordinary market rate of interest. A person who has capital from which he wishes to derive a revenue deliberates whether he should buy land or lend it out at interest.' He also suggests the 'superior security of land' offers considerable advantage.

---

in Australia were even lending people the money to attend such courses! But then the bubble burst. Property values dropped, capital gain turned into capital drain and investors experienced one of the major downsides to property – illiquidity. In other words, there isn't always a buyer when you need one.

Like all booms, the inexperienced masses got in at the tail end. For those who had bought property at rock-bottom prices before the term 'buy-to-let' was even invented, property was a genuine route to wealth creation. For the rest, it became a one-way ticket to trouble. Buy-to-let investors jumped in at the top of the housing bubble. Demand had created an oversupply, especially in the trendy executive rental market in certain cities. Falling rents and property values made it impossible to service the huge debt obligations. In the third quarter of 2008, 18,000 buy-to-let mortgages in the UK were in serious arrears, up 49% on the second quarter of the year.

Buying property is no longer a sure thing. Instead of struggling to get on the property ladder and having to purchase outside the preferred area, perhaps we will see a shift back to renting. The money that might have been consumed in fees, mortgage payments and maintenance could then be invested prudently for future financial growth.

YOUR THOUGHTS

EXPORT THE EXTRA

Only when the last tree has died and the last
river has been poisoned and the last fish has been
caught will we realise that we cannot eat money.
- CREE INDIAN SAYING

Smith suggests that a nation progresses when they use their resources to satisfy home demand and export the remainder. What's especially interesting about this idea is that China, an economic superpower, doesn't do it that way! For many reasons, China is a unique country, but the big one in relation to economics is the fusion between capitalism and communism. The average Chinese citizen is very conservative, hardworking and frugal. They have not been so afflicted by the materialistic malaise of the Western culture, at least not yet. In the TV documentary *This World: American Time Bomb* (2008), the contrast between the two countries couldn't have been starker.

A young Chinese couple were interviewed about their lives. Both worked in an electronics factory in Shanghai yet their home did not possess a single item that their manufacturing plant made. They saved half their income and their dream was to live in a quieter area and buy a car! The realistic and affordable aspirations of the Chinese have resulted in minimal internal demand, although that is changing.

Perhaps China has become an economic powerhouse because most of

---

FOOD FOR THOUGHT

Do your bit for the environment and teach your kids to do the same. Don't let the tap run while you are brushing your teeth, limit your use of plastic bags and if you must use them, re-use them over and over again. Instead of throwing things away, give them to a charity shop where they can be recycled for a good cause.

their manufacturing output is exported. In 2007, the Chinese exported more than they imported to create a trade surplus of $315,700,000,000. In contrast, the US imported more than they exported to create a trade deficit of $816,000,000,000. The UK was next, with a deficit of $175,400,000,000!

Smith believed that the natural progression was 'the greater part of capital of every growing society is first directed to agriculture, afterwards to manufacturers and last of all to foreign commerce'. He goes on to say that for most nations the steady movement from agriculture to manufacturing improves a nation's economic opulence, but eventually the improvements made in manufacturing filter back to agriculture. Perhaps the importance of land management, cultivation and food production, so often brushed aside in the name of progress, becomes glaringly obvious as Mother Nature extracts her revenge.

In the past China has thought little about deforestation to make way for its people and industry. In 2002 China embarked on a US$2.4 billion regeneration programme in an unprecedented effort to reverse the damage caused by their industrialisation. Wholesale logging has resulted in expanding deserts, chronic droughts and deadly flooding, which China hopes to stop by replanting 170,000 square miles – an area the size of California – over a ten-year programme.

YOUR THOUGHTS

THE IMPORTANCE OF
LONG-RANGE THINKING

Everybody, soon or late, sits down
to a banquet of consequences.
- ROBERT LOUIS BALFOUR STEVENSON,
Novelist, Essayist and Poet

Economically you can't argue with China's performance. The Chinese will be adversely affected by the sub-prime induced credit crunch of 2007–2009 simply because their key markets are in turmoil and demand will drop. With trillions of dollars in surplus, however, China will no doubt weather the storm far more comfortably than most. But it's not all rosy in the garden: lack of long-range planning regarding the environmental impact of their economic growth may not be a problem unique to China. What is unique, though, is their significant preference toward 'the male sex' and the social ramifications of a population control strategy that's gone badly wrong.

In 1979 the Chinese government introduced the controversial one-child family policy in an effort to stem the problem of rising population. At the time, China was home to a quarter of the world's population – squashed into just 7% of the world's arable land. Two-thirds of that population were under thirty years old and therefore entering their reproductive years. In response to that, the Chinese government made it illegal to have more than one child per family.

FOOD FOR THOUGHT

When you have a decision to make, it's important to take time to think about the long-range ramifications of your actions. Consider the people involved and what might change; think about the places or economic circumstances involved and how they could alter. Deliberately think of the most outrageous possibilities that could result from the choices you make today. If you can comfortably live with the consequences, even the bad ones, press on.

With a traditional preference toward male children anyway, this led to predictable results. Sex-selection abortion increased so the couple could try again for a boy. In rural areas female children have been killed, often drowned like unwanted kittens. For the lucky ones who did make it and arrived to parents unable to do the unthinkable, those girls were unregistered and effectively hidden from the authorities. It is also suggested that female children receive 'less aggressive' health treatment than their male counterparts.

The Chinese government has even acknowledged the potentially disastrous social consequences of this sex imbalance. Almost thirty years on, and the policy is said to have increased mental health problems and socially disruptive behaviour among men. Many men are now unable to marry and have a family. The scarcity of females has also resulted in kidnapping and trafficking of women for marriage and increased the numbers of commercial sex workers.

Economically, China is a dominant force but the consequences of the one-child policy are thought to be a real threat to future stability of the country. Considering the traditional prominence toward male children, it's hard to fathom how the Chinese government couldn't predict the shortage of women and the catastrophic consequences this would have. Taking time to future-pace your decisions can be crucial to success, as China is now finding out to its cost.

YOUR THOUGHTS

A CARROT IS ALWAYS
BETTER THAN A STICK

If the frontline people do count, you couldn't prove it by
examining the reward systems in most organisations.
- KARL ALBRECHT, Entrepreneur

Sadly, slavery or 'forced labour' is still prevalent in modern society. In 1997, police in New York discovered what the pressed dubbed 'The Jackson Heights Deaf-Mutes', a network of sixty-four Mexican immigrants, mostly deaf-mute, forced to sell trinkets in the city's subway system. The group, including children and pregnant women, was subjected to horrendous living conditions and frequent abuse. Like so many, these modern-day slaves were lured to their doom by the promise of well-paid jobs and good conditions.

According to US government estimates, between 700,000 and two million women and children are sucked into slavery every year around the world. In the US, forced labour exists in low-wage sectors without regulation, such as prostitution and sex services, domestic service, agriculture, sweatshop/factory and restaurant and hotel work. But this is not just a US problem, nor is it limited to women and children. Truly modern-day slavery, especially sex slavery of women and children, is a devastating example of how capitalism without ethics is pure evil.

In business, too, there are still throwbacks from a dominated workforce that Smith believes counter-productive to progress. He warns that ego

---

FOOD FOR THOUGHT

If you want something to be done really well in your business, reward it. Consider how you might share some of the profit with staff as an incentive toward better performance by rewarding innovations and new ideas on how to improve efficiency. Most people want to be recognised and rewarded for good performance and if others can see that reward, the performance of the entire operation is likely to improve.

WORDS OF WISDOM

Adam Smith writes, 'The experience of all ages and nations, I believe, demonstrates that the work done by slaves, though it appears to cost only their maintenance is in the end the dearest of any... Whatever work he does beyond what is sufficient can be squeezed out by violence only.'

---

can be bad for business, 'The pride of man makes him love to domineer, and nothing mortifies him so much as to be obliged to condescend to persuade his inferiors.' While this remains the norm in business, things are changing. Progressive management understands the economic and social benefits to be achieved from encouraging with a carrot rather than beating with a stick.

There can be no better example of progressive management than Ricardo Semler, head of Semco, a Brazilian business renowned for its radical industrial democracy and corporate re-engineering (see also page 8). To start with, Semler has, 'an added 30% faith in human nature', which translates to an extraordinary working environment. He trusts his people and encourages them to pursue their own personal goals ahead of their corporate goals.

Semler recognises that if you treat your staff like adults and give them the opportunity to seek personal satisfaction and challenge, the contribution they make to the business is far superior to any you might demand of them. It's a brave environment that has yielded a 900% growth in ten years, with the number of employees increasing from a few hundred to over 3,000, with a miniscule turnover of less than 2%.

As Smith reminds us, 'Avarice and injustice are always short-sighted.'

YOUR THOUGHTS

EMOTION IS BAD
FOR BUSINESS

If your desires be endless, your
cares and fears will be so too.
- THOMAS FULLER, Historian

In their lust for gold and silver, the Spanish plundered Peru and Brazil in the fifteenth century, believing the wealth would make Spain strong and prosperous. But, as Smith points out they, 'did not consider that the value of those metals has arisen chiefly from their scarcity'. In other words, Spain shot themselves in the foot because their determination to find gold created an over-supply and diminished its value.

By taking vast quantities of gold back to Spain, the plunderers created 'hyper-inflation', where prices increase rapidly as the currency loses its value. As recently as 1979, at least seven countries had an annual inflation rate of above 50% and more than sixty countries, including the UK and the US, had inflation in double digits. Today only a few countries have an inflation rate above 10%. Zimbabwe is the only one with hyper-inflation rendering the currency next to useless. In August 2008 the Z$100 billion dollar note was worth less than 8p.

Central banks may have the power to print more money when necessary, but as history will attest, creating it out of thin air (or shipping it in

---

FOOD FOR THOUGHT

Battening down the hatches during financial difficulties can make a bad situation worse. If you're in business, the natural reaction is to cut back on spending and marketing is often the first to go. Marketing should never be sacrificed under any economic conditions. Business can't survive unless it makes a sale. Instead, realise that most other businesses will retreat, leaving Swiss-cheese style holes in your market that a smart business person can take advantage of.

WORDS OF WISDOM

In book four Smith talks about political economy or the ability, *'to enrich both the people and the sovereign'*. Although he never refers to it as such, Smith goes on to explain the perils of fear and greed, and how corrosive both can be to economic prosperity.

from the other side of the world) serves only to devalue the existing currency and destabilise the economy.

Deflation isn't much better and is largely blamed for the Great Depression of the 1930s. A 'deflationary spiral' means falling prices lead to less production, lower wages and further drops in price, thus creating a vicious circle.

Often it's fear or greed that creates these vicious circles, with economic instruments powerless to stop them. Take Mr Hotdog owner, for example. He's got a thriving business: he's committed to marketing, buys the freshest rolls, best-quality meat and always provides a mouth-watering array of condiments. So, he decides to expand, but is convinced by his economist son that it's the worst possible time and he should instead batten down the hatches, cut back on expenses and ride out the recession. The father takes his son's advice and no longer buys the freshest rolls; he cuts back on his marketing and his condiments, and buys poorer-quality meat. Sure enough, business falls away. Only the business didn't suffer because of the economy, it suffered because he panicked and changed a winning formula.

Fiscal policy is one thing, but it's emotion, especially fear and greed, coupled with the business cycle that can make or break an economy.

YOUR THOUGHTS

OVER-TRADING EVENTUALLY
WEAKENS DEMAND

Make hay while the sun is shining.
- MIQUEL DE CERVANTES, Spanish Novelist and Poet

When it comes to sober men being dis-proportioned to their capital and a penchant for over-trading, few better examples exist than in the construction industry. According to estimates by *The Economist*, the total value of residential property in developed economies rose by more than $30 trillion between 2000 and 2005, an increase equivalent to 100% of their combined Gross Domestic Product (GDP).

A cacophony of 'experts' reassuring prospective investors that property was a sure bet, together with easy credit, meant suppliers of new property bent over backward to keep pace with demand. According to the Nationwide Building Society, the average UK home increased in value by 215% between the first quarters of 1997 and 2007. With figures like these, it's easy to see the attraction of property as more and more people sought to cash in on the boom.

Channel 4's *Cutting Edge* produced a report called 'Bobski the Builder', during which the cameras followed two building crews – one led by Jarek, an ex-chocolate salesman from Poland, and the other by Terry, a fourth-generation English builder. Granted, Jarek was part of the over-trading problem Smith warned about, as he was largely self-taught and

---

FOOD FOR THOUGHT

Decades of experience is no guarantee of quality, nor is relative inexperience necessarily a harbinger of impending disaster. Whatever professional services you are seeking, from a builder to an accountant, always ask for references and be sure to follow them up. If possible or appropriate, inspect the work and verify their involvement. The fact is, asking for a reference is more than most people will do and will more than likely scare off dubious practitioners.

clearly his previous experience in the confectionery business had limited value. Yet compared to Terry, he looked like a seasoned professional. Terry was every negative stereotype of the building industry rolled into one: he never turned up, the jobs took significantly longer than he promised, he was expensive and the end product was shocking. If anything, the documentary served to illustrate just how easy it is to prosper in a booming economy. It's unlikely either man will fare well in the subsequent bust.

Today a short cruise around any neighbourhood, from rural villages in Scotland to city suburbs with waterfront views, will prove, 'Before their projects can be brought to bear, their stock is gone and their credit with it.' In late 2008 many building sites are as deserted as the illustrious Mary Celeste!

In the UK an estimated £11.7 billion in housing projects was scrapped between 2007 and 2008, leading to increased unemployment as the construction industry contracted sharply. Easy credit disappeared, and with it access to mortgages for would-be buyers, as well as bridging finance for construction companies.

Smith warns of the perils of over-trading and the indiscriminate damage this will lead to, 'When the profits of trade happen to be greater than ordinary, over-trading becomes a general error among both great and small dealers.'

YOUR THOUGHTS

GET PAID ON TIME

*If you can't pay for a thing, don't buy it. If you
can't get paid for it, don't sell it. Do this, and you will
have calm and drowsy nights, with all of the good
business you have now and none of the bad.*
*- BENJAMIN FRANKLIN, Scientist, Inventor, Statesman,
Printer and Philosopher*

Smith suggests that in business trouble is unavoidable when, 'The
demand comes before the returns, and they have nothing at hand with
which they can either purchase money or give solid security for borrowing.'
Ask your average small business owner today about the constant
challenges they face and they would no doubt lament the same
debilitating problems that Smith was talking about, over 230 years ago.

But it's not just creditors who worry about being paid on time. For
thousands of UK businesses, especially small and medium operations,
getting paid is a constant thorn in their side as they find big-business
muscle continues to squeeze payment terms.

According to a survey conducted by Ciao Surveys on behalf of
Barclays Local Business Banking small businesses in the UK were owed
approximately £8.3 billion at the end of February 2008. The cost in time
alone to chase late payments equated to a staggering 544,640 wasted
working days. Almost 60% of small to medium enterprises experienced
problems, with a third admitting that late payment threatened the day-
to-day survival of the business. Just under 40% of small business owners

---

FOOD FOR THOUGHT

If you run a small or medium-sized business and find it difficult to
consistently get paid on time by customers, you may want to investigate
factoring and invoice discounting. It could work out cheaper and less
stressful for you than chasing your own payments.

── WORDS OF WISDOM ──

Smith states, 'It is not any scarcity of gold and silver but the difficulty which such people find in borrowing and which their creditors find in getting payment that occasions the general complaint of the scarcity of money.' Getting paid on time can cause problems for both lender and borrower.

confessed to using their own money to keep the business afloat while they waited for outstanding payments.

In an effort to alleviate this problem a number of innovative financial services have emerged, which were certainly not around in Smith's era. The first, factoring, involves a business selling their invoices to a third party. This means that all their invoices are then sent out with the factoring company's payment details and customers pay the factoring company directly. In return, the factoring company will pay the business up to 85% of the total value of the invoices, usually within two or three days. The factoring company, not the business, then chases any outstanding debt and charges a fee of between 3–5% of the total invoice for this service.

Invoice Discounting is very similar to factoring, except for one key difference. In factoring, the finance relationship is known to customers of the business. With invoice discounting, invoices are also sold to a third party but the original business still maintains control over its sales ledger and chases the debt itself. That way, the finance arrangement stays anonymous and the company can maintain and protect the business relationship. Both invoice discounting and factoring offer a cost-effective way to gain access to money tied up in unpaid invoices and improve cash flow.

── YOUR THOUGHTS ──

WAR IS LUCRATIVE

The first panacea for a mis-managed nation is inflation
of the currency; the second is war. Both bring temporary
prosperity; both bring a permanent ruin. But both are
the refuge of political and economic opportunists.
- ERNEST HEMINGWAY, Novelist and Journalist

Of those who have 'flourished greatly' perhaps oil services industry leader Halliburton stands head and shoulders above the rest. Prior to 2000, the company's CEO was none other than Vice President Dick Cheney. He retired to take the White House post on a severance package worth $36 million. Purely coincidence perhaps, but the second most powerful man in the world used to head a company that just happened to win huge contracts for rebuilding Iraq…

Logic would say there was probably a conflict of interest, but maybe they did a great job? Perhaps troops were looked after and protected, maybe Halliburton was frugal with US tax payers' dollars? Not according to several federal investigations. The House Committee on Oversight and Government Reform (HCOGR) conducts vigorous investigations to uncover waste, fraud and abuse to improve the operations of the federal government and examine wrongdoing in the private sector. Following dozens of hearings, the Committee identified abuse in federal spending as well as billions in misspent or mismanaged funds.

Investigations by the Committee documented wasteful spending by KBR, the former Halliburton subsidiary, under the contract to support

---

FOOD FOR THOUGHT

Don't believe everything politicians tell you, especially those with vested financial interests. As a society we all need to question authority far more than we do and remember that any and every argument can find supporting evidence. The Intelligence Community call this 'cherry picking', where statistics and facts are taken out of context to support a claim.

the troops and the contract to Restore Iraqi Oil (RIO). During a hearing in February 2007, the Committee learned that the Defence Contract Audit Agency (DCAA) identified over $10 billion in questioned and unsupported costs in Iraq, with $2.7 billion from the two KBR contracts alone.

Earlier Committee investigations found specific examples of unchecked spending by KBR, such as billing taxpayers $45 for a case of soda and $100 to wash a bag of laundry, inflating costs for gasoline delivery and abandoning new trucks that had broken down instead of maintaining them.

In the documentary 'Iraq for Sale: The War Profiteers' (2006) countless former employees blew the whistle. Military personnel replaced by contractors on inflated salaries, 5-star accommodation while the troops bunked in cramped tents, $75,000 trucks being destroyed because of a flat tyre… One former KGB/Halliburton truck driver described how wrongly ordered equipment, computers still in boxes and even new vehicles would be taken to 'burn pits' and set alight so the company could claim the loss and get more money. The evidence compiled was so shocking that director Robert Greenwald was invited to testify before Congress.

Halliburton may not have been the only contractor to profit from warbut the powerful and influential contacts make it especially distasteful.

YOUR THOUGHTS

FOCUS ON QUALITY

Quality is never an accident; it is always the
result of high intention, sincere effort, intelligent
direction and skilful execution; it represents the
wise choice of many alternatives.
- WILLIAM A. FOSTER, US Marine

Smith believed that as people became more and more specialised in particular tasks, a corresponding improvement in innovation and quality would follow. In truth, it didn't always work out like this. During the years after World War II there was increased demand for US manufactured goods. Despite their improved 'productive powers', this increase in demand did not lead to improved quality. Instead, gig manufacturing became complacent and quality dropped.

Meanwhile, on the other side of the world, the situation was very different. The war had devastated Japan and the Japanese needed to rebuild both production and their manufacturing reputation. In 1947, Douglas MacArthur and the US State Department sent W. Edward Deming to Japan to assist in this. Deming had worked with Walter Shewhart of the Bell Telephone Company during the 1930s. Shewhart had a theory: that product control could best be managed by statistics. Using this idea, Deming later developed a process that alerted managers of the need to intervene in the production process.

Japan was keen to improve its 'productive powers', listened intently

---

FOOD FOR THOUGHT

If you run a business, stay focused on quality. Test the systems in your own business at least once every six months. Call your business anonymously and place an order. How long did it take to arrive, what condition was it in? Step into your customers' shoes and test your own business to highlight areas where quality improvement would be beneficial.

to Deming and readily adopted his methodology. The focus on quality and craftsmanship naturally suited the Japanese cultural psychology for Deming's philosophy went beyond statistical quality control and encouraged building quality into the product at all stages, a process which became known as 'Kaizen' and is still used today in many Japanese companies, such as Toyota. Before the global crisis took off in 2007, Toyota's attention to quality and process efficiency made them hard to beat. In December 2008, the same company stunned the car industry by predicting their first operating loss for seventy-one years. This shock announcement indicated the severity of the economic downturn because if Toyota, one of the most efficient car manufacturers in the world, could not make money then what chance did the others have?

In 1960, Prime Minister Nobusuke Kishi, acting on behalf of Emperor Hirohito, awarded Dr Deming Japan's Order of the Sacred Treasure. The citation on the medal recognises Deming's contribution to the country's industrial rebirth and its worldwide success. By the early 80s Japanese products, particularly automobiles and electronic products, were far superior in quality to those created in the US. Today Japan remains world-famous for its manufacturing prowess. With the help of W. Edward Deming, Japan was able to 'augment its annual produce to the utmost' and make a significant difference to the wealth and prosperity of the nation.

YOUR THOUGHTS

WHEN IS CHEAP TOO CHEAP?

The only thing necessary for the triumph
of evil is for good men to do nothing.
- EDMUND BURKE, Political Theorist and Philosopher

Individuals and business should seek financial efficiency at all times. To illustrate the point, he goes on to explain, *'The tailor does not attempt to make his own shoes, but buys them off a shoemaker. The shoemaker does not attempt to make his own clothes, but employs a tailor.'* Business is a shortcut to a solution. If a Law degree could be obtained from the back of your Cornflakes packet in the morning, you probably wouldn't go to the expense of hiring a lawyer. Similarly, if you could buy a fantastic chocolate cake for less than the time and ingredients required to make it, it's an inefficient use of your resources not to buy it.

The problem with this idea is that it doesn't take the true price into consideration! The price of a product is not just the numbers on a swing ticket, it's the social and environmental price paid for getting that product or service to market. For example, how is it possible for Young's Seafood to transport Scottish langoustines 12,000 miles to Thailand to be shelled and then brought back for sale? Why are we offered Kenyan green beans in our local supermarket? Because, as Smith himself points out, *'wages of labour are very low, so the profits of*

FOOD FOR THOUGHT

Next time you're browsing in your local mega-discount retailer and marvelling how they can possibly provide such rock bottom prices, spare a thought for the child labour and sweat shop inhabitants almost certainly contributing to its manufacture. Imagine your own child or a family member having to work in such conditions and ask yourself if it's really worth that price.

> **WORDS OF WISDOM**
>
> Adam Smith says that, 'It is the maxim of every prudent master of a family never to attempt to make at home what it will cost him more to make than to buy'. Economic prudence, therefore, states that individuals and business should seek financial efficiency at all times.

stock are very high in ruined countries.' Also, we choose to turn a blind eye to it because we love a bargain!

As I've said before, the biggest challenge with The Wealth of Nations is that it fails to take human nature into account, which by all accounts is a serious mistake. There are enough examples, even in this book, to demonstrate the morally questionable practices that exist because of capitalism. Free enterprise can be a valid economic system, but this is on the assumption that human beings will not exploit each other, that the strong will not take advantage of the weak, and unfortunately that assumption is misplaced – even in the twenty-first century, perhaps especially in the twenty-first century! Capitalism without decency, humanity and moral conscience is tantamount to evil, whatever century you choose to examine.

Smith ends his point with an interesting and still-relevant observation, 'Our merchants frequently complain of the high wages of British Labour as the cause of their manufacturers being undersold in foreign markets, but they are silent about the high profits of stock. They complain of the extravagant gain of other people but they say nothing of their own.'

> **YOUR THOUGHTS**

WHEN IS ENOUGH, ENOUGH?

Five enemies of peace inhabit with us – avarice,
ambition, envy, anger and pride; if they were to be
banished, we should infallibly enjoy perpetual peace.
- FRANCESCO PETRARCH, Italian Scholar

For a start, I find it hard to accept that no human wisdom can foresee the benefits or misfortunes of certain choices and events. There were, for example, plenty of people who predicted the financial crisis that began in 2007, but they were inside the industry. As such, they were part of the problem, not the solution, and even if one or two genuinely warned of impending disaster, it's highly unlikely the powers that be, the ones reaping huge financial rewards, wanted to listen. Surely someone in China's elite figured that a traditional preference toward male children, coupled with a one-child family policy, might cause a serious gender imbalance?

Smith specifically related his comments to what he refers to as the two greatest and most important events recorded in the history of mankind: the discovery of America and the passage to the East Indies by the Cape of Good Hope. Yet even Smith, with his optimistic exuberance for capitalism, recognises that advancement and prosperity are not shared by all: 'The policy of Europe has very little to boast of... Folly and injustice seem to have been the principles which presided over and directed

---

FOOD FOR THOUGHT

There's no evidence that companies that grow rapidly do better than those who don't. If you run a business, your role in society is far greater than just the generation of revenue: you support communities and provide jobs and stability for others. Instead of focusing on growth, turn your attention to profitability, quality, improved customer experience and increasing staff morale and then enjoy the business you've created.

WORDS OF WISDOM

Smith asks, 'What benefits or what misfortunes to mankind may hereafter result from great events, no human wisdom can foresee. By uniting the most distant parts of the world to relieve one another's wants, to increase enjoyment and encourage industry the general tendency would seem to be beneficial.'

---

the first projects of establishing those colonies; the folly of hunting after gold and silver mines, and the injustice of converting the possession of a country whose harmless natives, far from having ever injured the people of Europe, had received the first adventurers with every mark of kindness and hospitality.'

I understand Smith's passion for a free market economy. On many levels, it is a solid and sound system: those who are not afraid of hard work and want to better their position, providing more for their family, should be encouraged to do so. Increasing business efficiencies and delivering a product or service to a willing market is essential. As a result, a social and economic system should always reward effort. But when is enough, enough?

Profiteering at the expense of other human beings is not acceptable, not in Smith's time and not today, but sadly, as he himself points out, 'Whenever there is great property, there is great inequality. For one very rich man there must be at least five hundred poor.' Whether we like it or not, admit it or not, that inequality will never alter while we choose to ignore it when it suits us.

YOUR THOUGHTS

CONCLUSION

Adam Smith's *The Wealth of Nations* is widely cited as the founding document of industry and classical economics. What's most striking about this old treasure is just how little has changed. The Enron collapse of 2001 followed almost exactly the evolution of the Mississippi Bubble of 1720. We look at the world and see change, increased violence, environmental concerns, wars, famine, boom-and-bust cycles and stock-market euphoria followed by widespread panic. There's a sense that the world is somehow getting worse. And yet nothing much has changed at all. We're concerned about binge drinking and yet Smith talks about the multitude of alehouses and the 'disposition to drunkenness among the common people'. At the time of writing the world is in financial crisis. This particular crisis, while exceptionally bad, is not the first and it probably won't be the last. Adam Smith warns of the need for banking regulation, a prediction as relevant today as it was then.

He also writes of, 'the extraordinary expense of fuel' and yet it's still a current issue. We are also warned about the 'Avarice and ambition of the rich, hatred of labour and the love of present ease and enjoyment' – both still major themes in our society. Look at the banking chiefs, city traders and benefit queues, if you don't believe me!

If we forget religious storytelling for a moment and concentrate on the facts, we can prove that the world has existed for millions of years, with human beings evolving for a great many of them. In the continuum of that life- span we are still infants and so the repetition of history makes sense. Like a small child, we repeat a task over and over until finally our little brain thinks, 'Mmm this hurts, I think I might stop.' Unfortunately, as we brace ourselves for what many are calling Financial Armageddon, our collective penchant for hitting our head off the same wall seems far from over.

Sadly evolutionary psychology shows that we are still driven by the same basic emotions of our cave-dwelling ancestors. Fear and greed still drive human nature; corruption by those in positions of power is expected. Lies and broken promises become the staple diet of politics and the selfish pursuit of all things 'me' is admired. Bigger houses, faster cars, more clothes and bigger TVs go hand in hand with more stress, more envy, less love, less time, shallower relationships and greater isolation. Which begs the question – what's it all for? Are we evolving in the right direction?

Perhaps the financial crisis of 2007–2009 will end up becoming the wake-up call that the Western world so desperately needs. Maybe it will herald a much-needed psychological adjustment in the way we view and live our lives. Perhaps home entertainment systems will be substituted with conversation and a desire for connection with family and friends replace the selfish lust for money at any cost. We might even start to reverse the damage we have collectively done to this planet and realise that plundering resources in the name of profit for another trinket or toy isn't anything like as rewarding as being able to swim in clean oceans, watch the sun set on a winter's evening or walk through the countryside with your family. To paraphrase the American rock band R.E.M: Maybe the end of the financial world as we know it will have us all feeling just fine ... eventually!

REFERENCE MATERIAL

IDEA 1
Facebook 'costs businesses dear', BBC News Online, 11 September 2007.

IDEA 2
The History of the Laser by Mario Bertolotti.

IDEA 3
Lecture: 'Leading By Omission' by Ricardo Semler, Massachusetts Institute of Technology
(MIT) Sloan School of Management, 22 September 2005.

IDEA 4
Lecture: 'Leading By Omission' by Ricardo Semler, Massachusetts Institute of Technology
(MIT) Sloan School of Management, 22 September 2005.
The American Future: A History by Simon Schama, p. 308.
Transcript of Jimmy Carter's Address to the Nation on Energy, Miller Centre of Public Affairs, University of Virginia, 18 April 1977.
Influence Science and Practice by Robert B. Cialdini, 22 September 2005.

IDEA 5
1833 Factory Act, The National Archives.
Frames of Mind: The Theory of Multiple Intelligences by Dr H. Gardner.

IDEA 7
The American Future: A History by Simon Schama, p. 349.

IDEA 8
'Mint warns against melting coins', BBC News website, 12 May 2006.
'Six billion copper coins missing' by Peter Stebb, *This Is Money,* 24 April, 2007.

IDEA 10
'King attacks banks delay in clearing cheques' by Philip Thornton, *Independent,* 17 June 2004.
'Waiting time for cheques to clear to be cut from next year', *Daily Telegraph* website, 14 November 2006.
'Bank deposit guarantee raised to £50,000 after Brown bows to pressure' by Patrick Hosking, *The Times,* 3 October 2008.

IDEA 11
Management Powertools: A Guide to 20 of the Most Powerful Management Tools and Techniques Ever Invented by Harry Onsman, p. 23.

IDEA 12
'The week when the rumour mongers ran the asylum' by Siobhan Kennedy, *The Times,* 20 March 2008.
'No charges expected in HBOS share price inquiry' by Martin Flanagan, *Scotsman*, 23 June 2008.
The Ascent of Money: A Financial History of the World by Niall Ferguson, p. 613.
'Coca-Cola ad trades on secret recipe' by Mark Sweney, *Guardian*, 7 July 2008.

IDEA 14
'BA hit by record £270m price-fixing fines' by Steve Hawkes, *The Times*, 1 August 2007.
'Office of Fair Trading charges British Airways executives with price-fixing' by Michael Herman, *The Times*, 7 August 2008.
'BA and Qantas fined millions for price-fixing' by Sophie Tedmanson, *The Times*, 28 October 2008.
The Ascent of Money: A Financial History of the World by Niall Ferguson, pp. 1
    69–172.

IDEA 15
The Great Game of Business by Jack Stack, pp. 1, 2 and 3.
Management Powertools: A Guide to 20 of the Most Powerful Management Tools and Techniques Ever Invented by Harry Onsman, p. 162.

IDEA 16
The 75 Greatest Management Decisions Ever Made… And Some of the Worst by Stuart Crainer, p. 194.

IDEA 17
'Average cost of bringing up a child to 21 reaches £180,000' by Rebecca Smithers, *Guardian*, 10 November 2006.

IDEA 20
HM Treasury Press Release: 'Graham Review of the small firms loan guarantee', 17 February 2004.

IDEA 21
'Unemployment: A Mental Health Issue', The Jobs letter No. 24, 9 September 1995.
'Raised on Welfare, the "Why Bother?" generation that doesn't want to work' by Benedict Brogan, *Daily Mail,* 21 April 2008.
'Meet the families where no one's worked for THREE generations – and they don't care' by Sadie Nicholas and Diana Appleyard, *Daily Mail*, 21 March 2008.

IDEA 23
'I never believed I was worth my $2.3 million bonus' by David Cohen, *Evening Standard,* 20 October 2008.
'Bank Governor Mervyn King launches unprecedented attack on "unattractive" City bonus culture' by Simon Duke, Daily Mail, 29 April 2008.
The Ascent of Money: A Financial History of the World by Niall Ferguson, p. 5.

IDEA 24
National Lottery website: Frequently Asked Questions.
Camelot Press Office: 'Key Facts about The National Lottery', 31 March 2007 (figures correct as at 7 July 2008).

IDEA 25
The Ascent of Money: A Financial History of the World by Niall Ferguson, pp. 176, 185 and 190
The Black Swan: The Impact of the Highly Improbable by Nassim Nicholas Taleb, p. 130.

IDEA 26
'Free Agent Nation' by Daniel H. Pink, *Fast Company,* Issue 12, September 1997.

IDEA 27
Credit Action Debt Facts and Figures, compiled 1 December 2008.

IDEA 28
'Would you pass the 11-plus?', BBC News Online, 27 March 2006.

IDEA 29
The Ascent of Money: A Financial History of the World by Niall Ferguson, pp. 278, 279 and 280. Grameen Bank website.

IDEA 31
'The Credit Card Industry: A History' by Lewis Mandell, p. 26
Credit Action Debt Facts and Figures, compiled 1 December 2008.
'Barclay chief's gaffe recalls Ratner howler' by Bill Wilson, BBC News Online, 17 October 2003.

IDEA 32
The Ascent of Money: A Financial History of the World by Niall Ferguson, pp. 246, 259 and 267.

IDEA 33
'Northern Rock besieged by savers', BBC News Online, 17 September 2007.
'£50bn bid to save UK banks' by Patrick Wintour, Jill Treanor and Ashley Seager, *Guardian,* 8 October 2008.
The Ascent of Money: A Financial History of the World by Niall Ferguson, p. 237

IDEA 34
The Ascent of Money: A Financial History of the World by Niall Ferguson, pp. 227 and 228.

IDEA 35
The Ascent of Money: A Financial History of the World by Niall Ferguson, p. 153.
Office of National Statistics figures: RP04 Retail Prices Index.
'Economy tables: Economic growth, interest rates and inflation history, unemployment', *Thisismoney.co.uk*, 4 December 2008.

IDEA 36
'UK manufacturing in sharp decline', BBC News Online, 9 December 2008.
'The facts about UK manufacturing', BBC News Online, 18 March 2002.

IDEA 37
'UK savings rate sinks to 49-year low as growth falters' by David Prosser, *Independent*, 28 June 2008.
I.O.U.S.A: One Nation. Under Stress. In Debt by Addison Wiggin and Kate Incontrera, pp. 43 and 72.

IDEA 38
Floor Statement: Senate Budget Committee Chairman Kent Conrad (D-ND).
During Floor Debate on FY 2009: Senate Budget Resolution, 12 March 2008.
Credit Action Debt: Facts and Figures, compiled 1 December 2008.
I.O.U.S.A: One Nation. Under Stress. In Debt by Addison Wiggin and Kate Incontrera, p. 82.
The American Future: A History by Simon Schama, p. 308.

IDEA 39
Credit Action: Debt: Facts and Figures, compiled 1 December 2008.
'Runaway debts leave thousands high and dry', *Telegraph*, 26 July 2006.
The Ascent of Money: A Financial History of the World by Niall Ferguson, p. 59.

IDEA 40
United States Postal Service: Postal News Press Release: New Study Reveals 724,000 'Americans Rely On Ebay Sales For Income', 21 July 2005.
''Virgin Mary'' toast fetches $28,000', BBC News Online, 23 November, 2004.
eBay.co.uk Media Centre Fast Facts: About eBay.

IDEA 41
The Ascent of Money: A Financial History of the World by Niall Ferguson, pp. 39 and 40.
'Competition Commission to investigate doorstep lending', Fair Investment website, 22 April 2005.
Competition Commission: Home Credit inquiry Final Report, 28 April 2006.

IDEA 43

'China Begins Huge Reforestation Effort', Xinhua News Agency, 15 May 2002.
I.O.U.S.A One Nation. Under Stress. In Debt by Addison Wiggin and Kate Incontrera, p. 66.
CIA World Fact Book 2007: World Trade Imbalances.

IDEA 44

The Effect of China's One-Child Family Policy after 25 Years by Therese Hesketh, Ph.D., Li Lu, M.D. and Zhu Wei Xing, M.P.H.
The New England Journal of Medicine: Vol. 353, 15 September 2005.

IDEA 45

Cornell University ILR School: 'Hidden Slaves: Forced Labor in the United States', September 2004.
'7 Charged in N.Y. Ring Exploiting Deaf Immigrants' by John J. Goldman, *Los Angeles Times*, 21 July 1997.
Lecture: 'Leading By Omission' by Ricardo Semler, Massachusetts Institute of Technology (MIT) Sloan School of Management, 22 September 2005.

IDEA 46

The Ascent of Money: A Financial History of the World by Niall Ferguson, p. 108.
'Zimbabwe's inflation rate surges to 231,000,000%' by Chris McGreal, *Guardian*, 9 October 2008.

IDEA 47

'The global housing boom', *The Economist*, 16 June 2005.
'The bubble bursts', *The Economist*, 10 April 2008.
Channel 4 *Cutting Edge*: 'Bobski the Builder', broadcast 16 October 2008.

IDEA 48

Barclays Media Centre Press Release: 'Leap year woes: small businesses will spend the extra day chasing late payments of £8.5 billion', 29 February 2008.

IDEA 49

Committee on Oversight and Government Report: 'Reform Waste, Fraud, and Abuse Identified by Oversight Committee Investigations', 3 October 2008.
Documentary: 'Iraq for Sale: The War Profiteers' by Robert Greenwald, 29 October 2006.

IDEA 50

'Quality and Total Quality Management', *Encyclopedia of Management*, ed. Marilyn M. Helms, Gale Cengage, 2006.
'Toyota braced for historic loss', BBC News Online, 22 December 2008.
W. Edward Deming, Wikipedia website.

INDEX